El Dorado
THE GOLD OF ANCIENT COLOMBIA

from
El Museo del Oro,
Banco de la República
Bogotá, Colombia

Distributed by
New York Graphic Society for
The Center for Inter-American Relations
and
The American Federation of Arts

El Dorado
THE GOLD OF ANCIENT COLOMBIA

from
El Museo del Oro,
Banco de la República
Bogotá, Colombia

The Center for Inter-American Relations

The Center for Inter-American Relations conducts educational programs in the visual arts, music, literature and public affairs in order to enlarge our knowledge and appreciation of the cultural heritage as well as the political, economic and social problems of the Western Hemisphere.

The Center is a non-profit, tax-exempt membership corporation financed by foundation support, membership dues, and corporate and individual gifts.

The American Federation of Arts

The American Federation of Arts is a national, non-profit, educational organization, founded in 1909, to broaden the knowledge and appreciation of the arts of the past and present. Its primary activities are the organization of circulating exhibitions which travel throughout the United States, and the fostering of a better understanding among nations by the international exchange of art.

The paperbound edition of this publication served as the catalogue of an exhibition supported by a grant from The National Endowment for the Arts.

The clothbound edition is distributed for the Center for Inter-American Relations and the American Federation of Arts by New York Graphic Society, Greenwich, Connecticut 06830.

International Standard Book Number 0-8212-0626-5 (clothbound edition)
Library of Congress Catalog Card Number 74-9053

Design and format by Leon Auerbach

Photography by Luiś F. Barriga G., Bogotá and El Museo del Oro, Bogotá

Printed by Jaylen Offset Lithography, New York
Typography by Cyber-Graphics, Inc., New York

Preface

The Center for Inter-American Relations and The American Federation of Arts are exceptionally proud to present this exhibition of pre-Columbian gold and various related ceramics and stone from the collections of El Museo del Oro, Banco de la Republica, Bogotá, Colombia. After its initial presentation at the Center in New York in the spring of 1974, the exhibition will travel to major museums throughout the United States and Canada for a period of two years. The selection and organization of the show was done by Julie Jones, Curator of the Museum of Primitive Art in association with the staff of El Museo del Oro. The exhibition and publication were generously aided by a grant from the National Endowment for the Arts.

Needless to say, many people in Colombia and the United States were involved in the preparation of the project. We are profoundly grateful to them all, but we wish to express our gratitude in particular to Julie Jones of the Museum of Primitive Art, New York, Dr. Luís Barriga del Diestro, Administrative Director, Mrs. Clemencia Plazas del Nieto, Curator and the staff of El Museo del Oro in Bogotá. Without their knowledge and devotion the exhibition would literally not have been possible.

We are also deeply indebted to their Excellencies Ambassador Douglas Botero-Boshell, Colombian Ambassador to the United States, Ambassador Aurelio Caicedo Ayerbe, Ambassador of Colombia to the United Nations, Mr. Sidney Hamolfski, Cultural Attaché, American Embassy, Bogotá, Dr. German Botero de los Rios, Gerente General, Banco de la República, Bogotá, the Colombian Information Service and Avianca Airlines.

JOHN M. CATES, JR.   WILDER GREEN
President   *Director*
Center for Inter-American Relations   *American Federation of Arts*

Contents

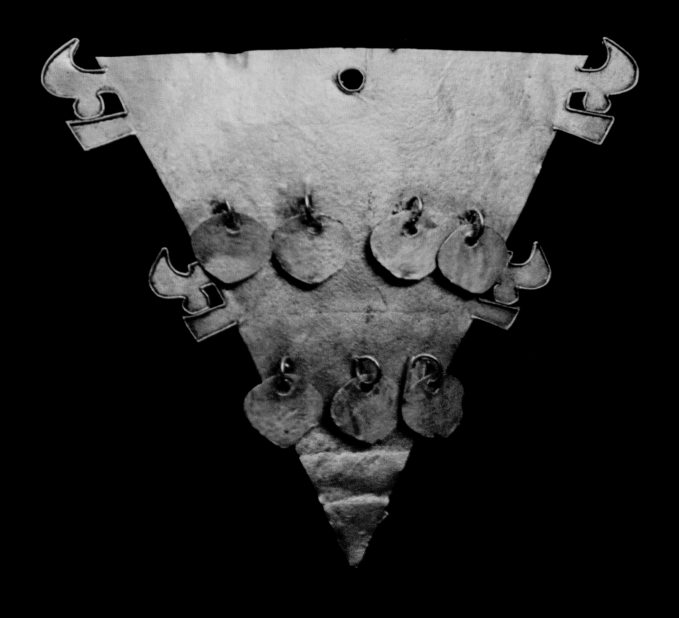

Gold
and the
New World

JULIE JONES
CURATOR
THE MUSEUM OF PRIMITIVE ART

In the discovery and conquest of the New World there is a special and very meaningful place for gold. To the vivid imagination of late medieval Europe, gold was the ready symbol of wealth and power; the search for it was part of New World history even before the thought of sailing westward to the Indies brought a gleam to the eye of Christopher Columbus. The Age of Discovery itself, to which the discovery of America notably belongs, begins with a story of gold. In the early 15th century, Europe traded for gold in the port cities of North Africa, where gold dust, carried across the Sahara in Moorish caravans, reached the hands of European merchants. In 1415, one of the trading ports, the Moroccan city of Ceuta, fell to an invading force from Portugal. The Portuguese were astonished at the amount of gold they found in Ceuta and were soon to begin sea voyages down the coast of Africa in an effort — among others — to reach the source of the gold. These 15th century Portuguese sea voyages to the west coast of Africa are considered to mark the beginning of what is known as the Age of Discovery.

Although the search for gold was not initially the whole aim of these voyages, within twenty-five years it was a most important part of the Portuguese effort in Africa. Horses, cloth, and brassware were traded for gold dust, ivory, and slaves. By the mid-15th century, Portugal controlled a substantial percentage of all the gold coming from Africa, and for the next hundred years they were a dominant force in the African gold trade. During the 1480's, a particularly dynamic period of Portuguese exploration and trade, the Genoese sailor Christopher Columbus was aboard Portuguese ships, sailing at least once to Africa. Columbus saw the great chests of gold dust which were sent back to Portugal and soon formulated a plan of his own for reaching an even more golden land, the fabled Indies, the rich realms of Asia.

Portugal was attempting to reach Asia by sailing around Africa; Columbus proposed to reach it by sailing across the western sea. He believed that by traveling westward he would reach Cipangu (Japan), the wealthy island kingdom described by the great traveler Marco Polo. Marco Polo had had this to say about Cipangu: "[It] is an island towards the east in the high seas, about 1,500 miles distant from the Continent . . . And I can tell you the quantity of gold they have is endless . . . the Palace of the Lord of that Island is entirely roofed with fine gold, just as our churches are roofed with lead" (Polo, 1903, v.2: 253-54). Such marvels were very real to 15th century Europe. Not only were the golden palaces of Cipangu well known, but the wealth of the Great Khan of Cathay (China) was familiar to those who read medieval travel accounts. The Great Khan's palace was reported to have halls covered with fine gold. A golden vine above his table had clusters of grapes all made of precious stones; peacocks made of gold danced and flapped their wings on solemn occasions. Columbus was so convinced that he would find the Great Khan of Cathay and the marvelous court, that he took a special ambassador to the court with him on his journey westward.

In the early fall of 1492, Christopher Columbus, sailing with three ships under the flag of Spain, successfully navigated the western sea and landed in the "islands of the Indies." His first concern was to locate Cipangu. Sailing restlessly among the new-found islands he looked for golden Cipangu and mighty Cathay. On the island now known as Cuba, the ambassador to the Great Khan was sent out, but no Great Khan was found. Columbus asked incessantly for gold; surely gold would lead him to the splendid palaces and great courts, to the emperors and kings. For two and a half months he sailed, but found little gold, until quite by chance one of his ships ran onto a coral reef off the island of Española.

The ship ran aground on Christmas eve in a calm sea. To empty the wrecked ship Columbus asked the help of a neighboring Indian chieftan. The shipwreck attracted many Indian onlookers and among them were a number who wanted to trade pieces of gold for the small brass hawks' bells the Europeans carried. At the sight of the Indian gold Columbus was very pleased, and the helpful Española chieftain, in turn, "was greatly delighted to see [Columbus] joyful and understood that he desired much gold, and he told him by signs that he knew where there was very much in great abundance near there, and that he should be of good cheer, for he would give him as much gold as he might desire" (Columbus, 1960: 124-28). Later, after feasting with the chieftain, "a large mask, which had great pieces of gold in the ears and eyes and in other places" was given to Columbus together with "other ornaments."

Although his mind's eye was firmly fixed on the splendor and riches of Cipangu and Cathay, Christopher Columbus was not unprepared for less dazzling realities. Sailing to Asia, he had prepared as for sailing to Africa. He had taken the same trade items the Portuguese had used in Africa — cloth, brassware, and glass beads. Columbus did not doubt that gold among the natives implied the nearby presence of a gold mine and he built a fort on Española of the remains of the wrecked ship. Some men were left behind to trade for gold and look for the gold mine. Cipangu and Cathay had perhaps eluded him, but he had found gold.

Three weeks after the discovery of gold Columbus returned to Spain. During the homeward passage Columbus wrote to his patrons, the Catholic Kings of Spain, Ferdinand and Isabella, telling them of the success of his voyage. He wrote of the innumerable people who lived on the newly discovered islands, and of the great many rivers that contained gold, of the mines of gold and other metals. This startling news was well received in Spain when Columbus was joyfully welcomed at court in the spring of 1493. The report of the voyage was published the month in which he reached the Spanish court, and by the year 1500 some twenty different editions of it had been published in Europe. The news spread quickly. The "islands of the Indies," the golden lands across the western sea, had won their first renown.

At the Spanish court plans were immediately made for a second voyage. Columbus warned that there should be strict control of "gold-hunting," for he said that eagerness in the search for gold would make the colonists neglect their other duties. In September of 1493, twelve hundred men set sail for the Indies intent upon converting the natives to Catholicism and on setting up a trading system for the Spanish crown. When the many eager colonists reached the island of Española two months later, the men Columbus had left behind were dead and the tiny fort destroyed. No gold mine was waiting. The Spaniards soon learned that there was no mine at all on Española. The gold which had been encountered initially and which the Indians had given away so generously, was alluvial gold that had been accumulating for years. In order to get enough gold to send to Spain, Columbus had to impose a tax on the Indian population of the island. The tax was to be paid in gold dust, or its equivalent in spun cotton, and it proved impossible to meet. Even when lowered by fifty per cent the Indians had difficulty meeting it.

Although the islands of the Indies did not immediately produce as much gold as expected, the Spanish sovereigns continued exploration and colonization. For Columbus's third voyage, in 1498, more orders were issued on the subject of "gold-hunting." Royal consent was needed in order even to look for a mine, a regulation which remained in effect until 1504. It was then modified and royal consent could be obtained for those who looked for and worked mines, if their claims were registered, and if they paid the proper tax. Taxes also were lowered. There had been a two-thirds tax on bullion, the tax then current in Spain, but to induce new development in the Indies a lower tax was found necessary. Between 1500 and 1504 the tax went down first to one-half, then to one-third, then to one-fifth, the famous *quinto* (royal fifth) of the Spanish crown. The *quinto* went into effect on February 5, 1504, and remained in effect in all of Spanish America until the 18th century. Collected on gold, silver, mercury, precious stones, and pearls, the *quinto* was a consistent and profitable source of income from the New World for three hundred years.

The image of the "islands of the Indies," created in Europe by Columbus' famous and well-published letter of 1493, is important to the discussion of gold. The first report about the Indies said the islands were rich in precious metals. "Incalculable gold" wrote Columbus. With a head full of medieval fantasies of splendid Asiatic courts and visions of chests full of African gold dust, Columbus could not think of gold in the relatively modest amounts he actually encountered. Years were to pass before incalculable wealth in precious metals was to come from the Indies, and even then it would be primarily in silver, yet at its beginning America was said to be a golden land and a golden land it would remain.

Columbus had invented American gold but it was left to others to find it. And find it they did, as if compelled to fulfill the great mariner's fantasy. There is no part of the subsequent discovery, conquest, and early colonization of the New World that is without its story of gold. Gold led Hernan Cortés to Mexico. Gold had been found among the natives along the coast of Yucatán, and the quest was on. Cortés sailed from Cuba in February of 1519. On November 9th of that year, he and his men reached the Aztec capital of Tenochtitlán, deep in the highlands of central Mexico. The great Aztec lord, Moctezuma, ruler of the most powerful Indian state ever to exist on the North American continent, was paralyzed with fear because he thought Cortés to be a god and he welcomed him into his city.

"And when [the Spaniards] were settled, they thereupon inquired of Moctezuma as to all the treasure of the city — the devices, the shields. Much did they tax him; with great zeal they demanded gold. And Moctezuma, upon this, proceeded to lead the Spaniards, who went surrounding and crowding about him as he went among them. He went at their head; they advanced with hands laid upon him, taking hold of him. And when they had arrived at the treasure house, called Teocalco, thereupon were brought out all the brilliant goods — the quetzal feather head fan, the devices, the shields, the golden discs, the devils' necklaces, golden leg bands, golden arm bands, golden head bands . . . they took all, all which they saw to be good." (Sahagun, 1955: 42-47).

14

23

The gold of Mexico, like that of Española, was alluvial gold. Once the accumulated wealth of the Aztec empire had been collected, divided, and enjoyed, there was no new source of gold in any quantity. Not until silver began to be mined in the early 1530's was Mexico to again produce precious metals in bulk; over ninety per cent of all the bullion shipped from the New World by the 1560's was silver. The Viceroyalty of Peru (Spanish South America) yielded the great quantities of precious metals, not the Viceroyalty of New Spain (territory north of the Isthmus of Panama). It was only after the conquest of Peru that the first great treasure fleet set sail for Spain.

The journey south to another continent — to the future Viceroyalty of Peru — was prefigured by tales of gold and golden cities, and the Spaniards were led on by them as surely as Columbus had been compelled onward by tales of the golden palaces of Cipangu. In 1531, one hundred and eighty Spaniards under the leadership of Francisco Pizarro found the legendary kingdom they had been seeking. Cities, royalty, emperor, gold, they found it all. The vast and powerful Inca kingdom surpassed even Moctezuma's realm in the brilliance of its gold and the gleam of its silver.

"The doorways of many buildings were elegant and much painted, and on them were placed precious stones and emeralds. Inside the Temple of the Sun and the palaces of the Inca kings the walls were plated with the finest gold, and carved with many figures all made of this metal and very fine . . . And in the rooms there were bunches of corn stalks made of gold and on the walls were sheep and lambs carved from gold, and birds and many other things. Besides this, they say that there was a great sum of treasure in pitchers and jars and pots, and many very rich mantles full of silver work and beads. Actually, no matter what I say, I cannot say enough of the wealth the Incas had in their royal palaces, in which there was great value, and where many silversmiths were kept to make the things I have mentioned and many others" (Cieza de Leon, 1554: 119-120).

In November of 1532 the Inca ruler, Atahuallpha, was ambushed and made prisoner by the Spaniards. Fearful that he would be put to death, he offered to buy his freedom. As ransom he offered "enough gold to fill a room twenty-two feet long and sixteen wide to a white line at half the height of the room, or half again his height. He said that he would fill the room to that mark with various pieces of gold — pitchers, jars, tiles and other things. Of silver he would fill that house twice full" (Xerez, 1917: 68). Atahuallpa met his ransom, but he was not set free. The enormous ransom did not save the Inca ruler's life. Nor did the great amounts of gold taken from the temples and palaces save the life of his kingdom. Atahuallpa was put to death three months after his ransom was melted down and divided among the Spaniards. The Inca territories were thoroughly ransacked and every bit of gold and silver was relentlessly searched out. Pizarro and his men left nothing — no gold, no silver, no kingdom.

The hoard of previous metal amassed with the collapse of Atahuallpa's rule was never again to be equalled in Indian America; the quest for gold among Indian kingdoms would never bring greater results, would never yield more treasure, would never reach such heights of fantasy. The drama which began in 1492 when Columbus first found gold among the Indians of Española culminated forty years later in the mountain kingdom of Inca Peru where gold covered temple walls, imperial palaces had golden furnishings, and every port held golden treasure. Could medieval Cipangu have been more marvelous?

Yet the search for gold continued still. Aztec Mexico had been rich, Inca Peru had been richer, other kingdoms would be even richer yet. Tales were heard of El Dorado, the Seven Cities of Cibola, the land of Quivira; where rumor of gold led them, the Europeans followed, and no rumor was more persistent than that of El Dorado: ". . . there is a lake in the land of this chief, onto which, placed in the middle of a well-made raft, he went a few times a year. He went naked but his body was covered from head to hands and feet with a kind of sticky turpentine on which much fine gold dust was scattered; the gold united with the turpentine and made a second skin of gold. In the morning sun of a clear day, when this sacrifice was performed, he was very brilliant. He would go to the middle of the lake and make offerings by throwing emeralds and pieces of gold into the water while he pronounced certain words. Then, washing his body with herbs like soap, the gold on his skin fell into the water and the ceremony ended. He would then leave the lake and put on his mantle" (Simon, 1953: 163).

The brilliant El Dorado, the Golden One, was pursued on the high plateau of central Colombia in the land of the Chibcha Indians. Rumor placed the fabulous ruler there first, but the Chibchas had no great amount of gold and El Dorado was not found. The search continued and the legend grew: in the land of El Dorado all the vessels were made of gold and silver; there were golden statues as big as giants; and everything there was in the land — birds, beasts, fish, trees, everything — had its counterpart in gold. The searchers pushed further and further east in dogged pursuit of the golden dream, and by the end of the 16th century, the English adventurer, Sir Walter Ralegh looked for El Dorado in Guiana which, he said, was "directly east from Peru towards the sea" and "it hath more abundance of gold than any part of Peru." (Ralegh, 1596: 11-12). Elusive and wary, the golden king of the golden land could not be found. El Dorado became the very substance of the earliest of American dreams, the belief in the existence and availability of great riches. Only in legend could El Dorado exist safely; in legend, the ultimate golden kingdom of the New World could not be conquered or despoiled.

In the first century and a half after the discovery of gold in the New World, one hundred eighty-one tons of gold and sixteen thousand tons of silver went officially (more is assumed to have gone unofficially) to Europe from the Spanish possessions in America. So great was this quantity of treasure that it influenced the power structure of Europe for centuries. It was of major importance to the growth and maintenance of the first global empire in the history of the world, the realm of the Hapsburg monarch Charles V, King of Spain, Catholic ruler of the Holy Roman Empire, Emperor of the Indies. "It is his Indian Golde that indaungereth and disturbeth all the nations of Europe, it purchaseth intelligence, creepeth into Councels, and setteth bound loyalty at liberty, in the greatest Monarchies of Europe" (Ralegh, 1596: 3 verso). It is small wonder, then, that all the masks, diadems, necklaces, arm bands, leg bands, crowns, ear plugs, nose rods, figures, disks, rings, pins, bracelets, bottles, ornaments, pots, plaques, pectorals, specters, and statues, were melted down into neat gold bars. Gold was needed to build new empires.

Bibliography

Early Sources

CIEZA DE LEON, PEDRO DE

1554 *Parte Primera de la Cronica del Perú*. En casa de Juan Steelsio, Anvers.

1880 *Segunda Parte de la Cronica del Perú*, edit. by Marcos Jimenez de la Espada. Madrid.

COLUMBUS, CHRISTOPHER

1960 *The Journal of Christopher Columbus*, trans. by Cecil Jane. Clarkson N. Potter, Inc., New York.

1961 *Four Voyages to the New World, Letters and Selected Documents*, trans. & edit. by Richard Henry Major, intro. by John E. Fagg. Corinth Books, New York.

COLUMBUS, FERDINAND

1959 *The Life of the Admiral Christopher Columbus by his Son, Ferdinand*, trans. & annotated by Benjamin Keen. Rutgers University Press, New Brunswick.

CORTÉS, FERNANDO

1908 *His Five Letters of Relation to the Emperor Charles V*, trans. & edit. by Francis Augustus MacNutt, 2 vols. A.H. Clark Co., Cleveland.

DÍAZ DEL CASTILLO, BERNAL

1908-16 *The True History of the Conquest of New Spain*, trans. by Alfred Percival Maudslay, 5 vols. The Hakluyt Society, London.

LOPEZ DE GOMARA, FRANCISCO

1964 *Cortés, The Life of the Conqueror by his Secretary*, trans. & edit. by Lesley Byrd Simpson, University of California Press, Berkeley & Los Angeles.

MANDEVILLE, SIR JOHN

1967 *Mandeville's Travels*, edit. by M.C. Seymour, The Clarendon Press, Oxford.

POLO, MARCO

1903 *The Book of Ser Marco Polo, the Venetian concerning the Kingdom and the Marvels of the East*, trans., edit. & annotated by Henry Yule, 3rd ed. rev., 2 vols. John Murray, London.

RALEGH, SIR WALTER

1596 *The Discoverie of the Large, Rich, and Bewtiful Empyre of Guiana, with a relation of the great and Golden Citie of Manoa (which the Spanyards call El Dorado) . . . performed in the yeare 1595 by Sir W. Ralegh Knight*. Robert Robinson, London.

SAHAGUN, BERNARDINO DE

1955 "The Conquest of Mexico," Book 12 of the General History of the Things of New Spain, Florentine Codex, trans. by Arthur J.O. Anderson & Charles E. Dibble. *Monographs of the School of American Research*, No. 14, pt. 13. Santa Fe.

SIMON, PEDRO

1953 *Noticias Historiales de las Conquistas de Tierra Firme en las Indias Occidentales*, vol. 2. Biblioteca de Autores Colombianos, Bogotá.

XEREZ, FRANCISCO DE

1917 Verdadera relación de la Conquista del Perú . . . en Las Relaciones de la Conquista del Perú. *Colección de Libros y Documentos referentes a la Historia del Perú*, vol. 5: 1-121. Lima.

Secondary Sources

BANDELIER, ADOLPH F.

1893 *The Gilded Man (El Dorado)*. D. Appleton & Co., New York.

BOVILL, E.W.

1968 *The Golden Trade of the Moors*, 2nd ed. Oxford University Press, London.

BOXER, C.R.

1969 *The Portuguese Seaborne Empire, 1415-1825*. Hutchinson & Co., London.

CRONE, G.R.

1969 *The Discovery of America*. Hamish Hamilton, London.

ELLIOTT, J.H.

1963 *Imperial Spain, 1496-1716*. Edward Arnold Pub. Ltd., London.

1970 *The Old World and the New, 1492-1650*.

Cambridge University Press, Cambridge.

GIBSON, CHARLES

1966 *Spain in America.* Harper & Row, New York.

HAMILTON, EARL J.

1929 Imports of American Gold and Silver into Spain, 1503-1660, *Quarterly Journal of Economics,* vol. 43: 436-72. Cambridge.

1929 American Treasure and the Rise of Capitalism (1500-1700), *Economica,* No. 27: 338-57. London.

1934 *American Treasure and the Price Revolution in Spain, 1501-1650.* Harvard University Press, Cambridge, Mass.

HARING, CLARENCE H.

1915 American Gold and Silver Production in the First Half of the Sixteenth Century, *Quarterly Journal of Economics,* vol. 29: 433-79. Cambridge.

1918 Early Spanish Colonial Exchequer, *American Historical Review,* vol. 23: 779-96. Lancaster.

1919 Ledgers of the Royal Treasurers in Spanish America in the Sixteenth Century, *Hispanic American Historical Review,* vol. 2: 173-187. Baltimore.

1947 *The Spanish Empire in America.* Oxford University Press, New York.

LOTHROP, SAMUEL K.

1938 *Inca Treasure as depicted by Spanish Historians,* F.W. Hodge Anniversary Publication Fund, vol. 2. The Southwest Museum, Los Angeles.

MORISON, SAMUEL ELIOT

1942 *Admiral of the Ocean Sea, A Life of Christopher Columbus,* 2 vols. Little, Brown & Co., Boston.

MULLER, PRISCILLA E.

1972 *Jewels in Spain, 1500-1800.* The Hispanic Society of America, New York.

O'GORMAN, EDMUNDO

1961 *The Invention of America.* Indiana University Press, Bloomington.

OLSCHKI, LEONARDO

1941 What Columbus saw on landing in the West Indies, *Proceedings of the American Philosophical Society,* vol. 84: 633-659. Philadelphia.

VICENS VIVES, JAIME

1969 *An Economic History of Spain,* 3rd ed. Princeton University Press, Princeton.

ZAHM, J.A.

1917 *The Quest of El Dorado, The Most Romantic Episode in the History of South American Conquest.* D. Appleton & Co., New York.

152

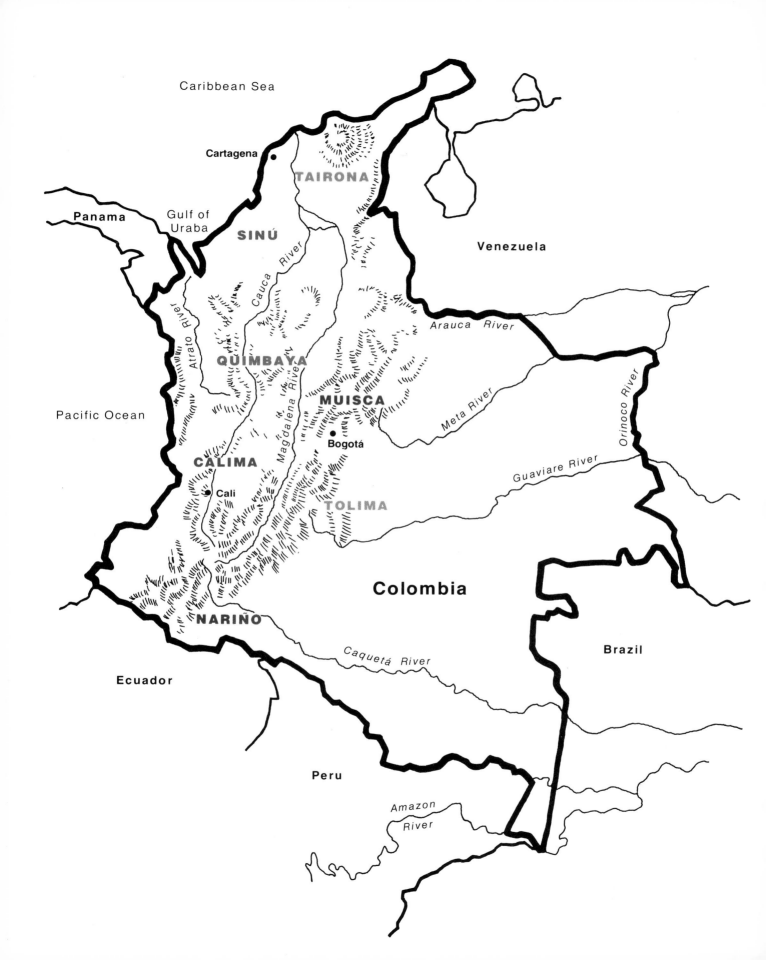

Caribbean Sea

Cartagena

TAIRONA

Panama

Gulf of
Uraba

SINÚ

Venezuela

Cauca River

Arauca River

Atrato River

QUIMBAYA

Pacific Ocean

Magdalena River

MUISCA

Meta River

Orinoco River

Bogotá

CALIMA

Cali

Guaviare River

TOLIMA

Colombia

NARIÑO

Brazil

Caquetá River

Ecuador

Peru

Amazon
River

Precolumbian Gold

JULIE JONES
CURATOR
THE MUSEUM OF PRIMITIVE ART

The area of the ancient New World which used gold extensively during ancient times is an area that today includes parts of Mexico, the Isthmian countries of Costa Rica and Panama, and the mountain regions of Colombia, Ecuador, and Peru in South America. It is an area of hundreds of thousands of square miles within which great variation in the manner and technique of gold use occurred. Gold was first worked on the American continents in the middle of the second millennium B.C. and its native use came to an end three thousand years later with the arrival of the Spaniards in the New World. While the extent and variety of the ancient gold work will never be fully known, as comparatively little of it remains intact, partial awareness of some forms is possible.

The first evidence for the working of gold in the New World has been found in that area of Andean South America which is today Peru. This important find of early gold was made in 1970 in the south highlands of Peru, at a site named Waywaca located just above the city of Andahuaylas. Numerous small pieces of thin gold foil — obviously worked by man — were found in a burial and an adjacent refuse deposit; also found were tools believed to be gold working tools, three small stone hammers and a larger stone anvil. Associated materials, dated by the radiocarbon method, reliably place gold and tools at 2000 B.C. (Grossman, 1974). Many centuries were to pass and much goldworking skill was acquired before the next group of goldwork now known from Peru is believed to have been produced. This group, dated stylistically to Chavin times in the first early millennium B.C., is astonishingly rich. It consists of personal ornaments — crowns, ear plugs, pectorals, nose ornaments, pins and the like, made of hammered sheet gold. Complex in design and very rare, these objects are the earliest works of art in gold known from the Americas (Lothrop, 1941, 1951).

The Chavin gold was apparently to be without peer on the American continents for some centuries as Peru had a long head-start in the manufacture and use of gold objects, if the present estimates of their inception elsewhere in the hemisphere are correct. Ecuador, just to the north of Peru, is believed to have begun using gold by the end of the first millennium B.C., as also is Colombia, Ecuador's northern neighbor. Panama and Costa Rica on the adjoining Isthmus of Panama apparently did not use gold for five hundred years more and the jump north to Mexico took place only towards the end of the first millennium A.D., at least two thousand years after gold was in significant use in early Peru.

Each of these ancient American goldworking areas — Peru, Ecuador, Colombia, Panama-Costa Rica, and Mexico — produced objects of distinct character and style. Although both representational and technological interaction took place within the larger gold using area, each region's goldwork was markedly individual. Peru, throughout its long history of gold manufacture, favored work by hammering; even the technical ability to cast metal did not change the predilection for repoussé gold surfaces. Ecuador too seems to have favored hammered work although Ecuadorian gold is poorly known and general statements about its character are therefore difficult to make. As a rule, gold objects were hammered objects, an indication of some form of overlap between the goldwork of ancient Peru and Ecuador. A relationship also seems to exist between the goldwork of northern Ecuador and southern Colombia. Colombia, as befits the land of El Dorado, produced goldwork which is one of the marvels of that ancient land.

The largest variety of style and diversity of technique found in the goldwork of any single ancient American area, are found in Colombia. Both hammered and cast objects abound. Formally they range from strong naturalism to marked stylization; the naturalistic styles produce the most straight-forwardly human figures known in Precolumbian gold, while stylization produces some of the most inorganic, patterned shapes. The adjoining Isthmian area, Panama and Costa Rica, is a region in which the ancient gold is unified by a similar iconography and a similar approach to material. This is the area known for the famous gold "eagles," bird form pendants of simplified outline, which were noted in 1503 on Christopher Columbus' fourth trip to the New World.

Mexico was the most northern producer of Precolumbian works of art in gold. Although influenced by the goldworking methods and styles of neighbors to the south, its works are unmistakably its own. Dependent on complex religious symbols for images, Mexican gold has more in common with contemporary Mexican works in other media than with the goldwork of areas further south. At a greater distance removed — all of the other gold areas lie one adjacent to the next — Mexican gold is the most "foreign" to the general spirit of Precolumbian gold. Peru, at the other end of the time and distance scale, was the area which apparently set the technical and artistic process of goldworking in motion, a seminal if somewhat confining role due to the highly traditional nature of ancient Peruvian art. Colombia, on the other hand, a middle land, was open to a multitude of influences and it also happened to be a region very rich in gold; thus it produced its many objects of diverse style and technique.

The Gold of Ancient Colombia

The event which served to bring ancient Colombian gold to public awareness was the four hundredth anniversary of Columbus' discovery of the New World. A fitting, if somewhat ironic occurrence, the Exposición-Histórico-Americana held in Madrid in 1892, was to present to the world's acclaim, for the first time since the 16th century, many original works made by the indigenous inhabitants of the Americas. The Exposición in honoring Columbus' discovery, was "to represent the condition of culture which was found on the continent of America by the first explorers" (Madrid, 1895: 23). Of the many European and American participants in the large exhibition, the Latin American republics were major contributors; Colombia's exhibit was outstanding among them, primarily because of its gold: "The Republic of Colombia presented perhaps the most brilliant of all the displays in the strictly American portion of the Exposition," commented one North American visitor. "The numerous magnificent specimens of native goldwork and their tasteful arrangement attracted the attention of all visitors. They also excited the admiration of those of antiquarian taste, from their novelty as well as for the perfection of their designs." (Madrid, 1895: 44).

The gold which did so much to attract attention in Madrid in 1892 included a group which is extraordinary to this day. It is the so-called *Treasure of the Quimbayas*, some 123 objects reportedly the gold contents of two ancient tombs. The tombs had been found in 1891 at a site named La Soledad, near the town of Filandia then in the Department of Cauca. The gold was purchased by the Colombian government, at the time assembling the exhibition material for Madrid, and hence the *Treasure of Quimbayas* made its way to Europe. While in Madrid the *Treasure* was given to the Queen Regent of Spain, Doña Maria Cristina, to be given by her in turn to the Museo Arqueológico Nacional. Now housed in Madrid's Museo de America, the *Treasure* consists of some of the most elegantly produced and sophisticated works of art in gold known from the New World. It is the most significant single group of ancient Colombian gold outside of Colombia.

The *Treasure of Quimbayas* is particularly notable for the quantity of

lime containers (or poporos as they are called in Colombia) included in it. Lime containers of varying sizes, shapes, and materials were used in South America to hold the lime used for the ritual of coca chewing. A small quantity of prepared lime, usually made from shell, was added to the dried coca leaf once in the mouth, in order to hasten the desired euphoric effect of the coca. In certain parts of South America such as Colombia, the lime containers, as an important part of the coca chewing paraphernalia, became luxury objects made of rich materials. Such luxury objects are the gold poporos of the *Treasure of the Quimbayas.* Some of the lime containers are extremely large in size, others — undoubtedly the most spectacular — are those made in the form of nude human figures. These cast figures whose hollow bodies form the vessel that holds the prepared lime, are of carefully balanced design and polished surface. Their bodies have been given a filled-out fleshiness and their facial features are altered only slightly by the addition of small nose ornaments. So compelling are these figural lime containers, that they are considered by many to be the greatest product of the ancient Colombian artist-goldsmith. As one admirer puts is, "they are true sculpture in gold," and are "a high point for the handling of gold as a material for sculpture in Pre-Columbian America" (Emmerich, 1965: 69). They have also become the fixed center around which ideas of "Quimbaya style" revolve.

In approaching "Quimbaya style" through the *Treasure of the Quimbayas,* however, problems arise immediately, problems which are symptomatic of the difficulties currently facing the study of ancient Colombian gold. The Quimbaya Indians were a historic Colombian tribe living to the west of the Cauca River in the Andean Central Cordillera; at the time of the Spanish Conquest, the Quimbayas were well known from their goldwork. A considerable amount of ancient gold, the so-called *Treasure* among it, has come from the area in which this historic tribe lived, and has been called Quimbaya without being identified in any way with the historic Quimbayas. As comparatively little archaeological work has been conducted in the Quimbaya area, (or for that matter in any of the Colombian goldworking areas), the cultural assignations of the ancient goldwork are often highly speculative.

In the past, the study of Colombia gold has been based on style groups outlined by geographic areas (Pérez de Barradas, 1954, 1958, 1966) but as investigation continues those style groups become increasingly difficult to maintain, leaving only geographic areas as significant categories. Previously too, tentative chronologies for the groups of gold have been provided by technical studies such as the chemical analysis of the gold content of the objects and by a detailing of methods of manufacture (e.g. Root, 1964). These chronologies are based on the assumption of increasing technological capability through archaeological time, perforce placing objects made by simpler means, i.e. objects made by hammering, at an earlier date than those of more complex manufacture, such as casting. A chronology of this sort does not allow for the continued use of, or preference for, simple techniques when more complex ones are available. Indeed the example of Peru — where precious metals were principally hammered even when casting techniques were available — indicates the limitations of the initial assumption. Other chronologies such as those formulated by stratigraphically produced cultural sequences anchored in time by such scientific processes as radiocarbon dating, are yet to take shape for most of Colombia's goldworking areas.

What is left then is geography; and Colombia's geography is multifaceted: "Colombia's extreme diversity of land configuration, meteorological features, and cultural developments has always defied any attempt at clear-cut description," writes noted Colombianist Gerardo Reichel-Dolmatoff. "Few countries in the world equal its environmental variety . . . In the course of its native history, this country has played a most varied but always important role. Its general location and particular complexity have made of Colombia both a gateway and a bottleneck, a cross-roads and a *cul-de-sac*, a centre of convergence and of diffusion, a splendid biological laboratory and a mosaic of ecological niches, where the struggle between human adaptive resources and natural environmental forces has continued up to the present day . . . All these factors tend, of course, toward extreme cultural diversity." (Reichel-Dolmatoff, 1965: 28-29).

Of the five natural geographic areas of Colombia, it is the Andean region which was chiefly identified with goldworking in ancient times. The Colombian Andes divide into three ranges forming the Western, Central, and Eastern Cordilleras; between them run the long, wide Cauca and Magdalena River valleys, home to many an ancient and modern man. Six of the seven ancient goldworking areas are found in the Cordilleras and adjacent valleys. The seven areas are currently identified as the Nariño, Calima, Quimbaya, Tolima, Muisca, Sinú, and Tairona. The Nariño, the most southerly of the seven areas, is the most newly discovered. Only in very recent years have important gold finds come from the area, an area which lies virtually across the Colombian Ecuadorian border. The name Nariño come from the Colombian Department of Nariño in which the archaeological area is located; the recent finds have been made around the highland towns of Pupiales and Ipiales. Notable among the finds have been nose ornaments of various open-work pattern embel-

26

lished with dangles, and small paired plaques in which a raised human or feline face appears in the middle (no. 1).

Somewhat further north on the Pacific side of the Western Cordillera near the headwaters of the Calima River, is the Calima area, famous for the quantity of ancient gold found there. Centered largely in the Department of the Valle de Cauca, the finds include hammered pectorals and funerary masks of considerable size and simple beauty. These objects are those thought to be among the "earliest" Colombian gold objects based on the technical simplicity of their manufacture. Made of sheet gold, the so-called funerary masks (no. 8) vary in the degree to which the features may be naturalistically rendered; while the pectorals (nos. 9-11), headdresses (no. 12) and arm ornaments (no. 13) which have the raised human faces in their center, faces almost hidden by the large nose and ear ornaments, are more standard in the depiction of facial features. The eyes, for instance, often the only feature visible on these small faces, seem to be shut, rendered simply as a line drawn through a slightly puffy eye lid, giving them a remote and inward looking quality.

Across the Western Cordillera in the middle Cauca River valley, is the Quimbaya area, named as has been noted for the Indian tribe which occupied part of the region at the time of the Conquest. The Quimbaya area has yielded some of the most refined and elegant gold objects known from Precolumbian America. Whatever their temporal placement the so-called Quimbaya objects are sleek and polished, conceptually more complex than most Precolumbian goldwork, while visually simpler. The human figure dominates, and it is an image almost devoid of anthropomorphic or heavily symbolic aspects. To the south of the Quimbaya region near the headwaters of the Cauca River, there is an area which has produced gold objects of strikingly different images — human figures with enormous bird beaks, the human aspect of the principal figure all but lost in the stylization of its form (nos. 92-93). This treatment of the human figure contrasts with other Quimbaya images where the figures have a fleshy substance and a human presence of marked insistence.

The Tolima area, on the eastern side of the Central Cordillera in the Magdalena River valley, is another gold area named for the Department in which the major finds have been made. Tolima is most particularly identified with an unusual kind of formalized pendant (nos. 95-97), the "winged" shape of which, although often called anthropomorphic, rather defies analysis. It seems to be a mixture of animal (perhaps bat) features, and inorganic patterns for the body of the creature. Such organic-inorganic combinations are unusual in Colombian gold, for all the numerous and complex human-animal images. The Tolima "winged" form pendants are arresting in the straight-forwardness of their design. All the parts are reduced to simple shapes and are completely visible, no element appears in front of, or obscures, any other. These pendants can, and indeed often do, succeed on the strength of their outline alone.

In high plateaus of the Eastern Cordillera, in the large basins of Bogotá and Tunja, is the Muisca area, home of the historic Chibchas. Muisca (or Chibcha) goldwork as a whole is the most stylistically and iconographically distinct of all of ancient Colombian gold. Not only do objects which can be described as having narrative content exist, such as the well known depiction of what is thought to be the raft of El Dorado, but warriors with trophy heads, coca chewers with poporos, large figures carrying smaller ones, and the like, are known, suggesting a visual source in a wider variety of life activities than is common for most ancient American gold. The Muisca approach to material too differs, for gold objects are essentially flat objects, flat objects with added surface detail. The multitude of charming offering figures of human image (nos. 108-119) are made of long, flat, slender shapes with eyes, nose, mouth, arms, ornaments, all additional small elements placed on top of the flat shape. Even pieces of three dimensional manufacture are made of "rounded" flat shapes, the metal seemingly unwilling to "bend." The surfaces of Muisca objects are not polished, smooth surfaces — which do so much to catch and reflect light — as so frequently found elsewhere. In contrast to the easy visibility of the Tolima objects just mentioned, for instance, Muisca objects do not reveal themselves at a glance; they demand close attention from the viewer.

The Sinú area, located primarily along the middle course of the Sinú and San Jorge Rivers, is the gold area which in Colombia lies closest to the Isthmus of Panama. The gold of this area is to some degree associated with an archaeological culture of some complexity; the biggest ancient earth mound yet known in Colombia for example is also associated with this culture. Sinú gold makes particular use of openwork light-pierced patterns, either as the major portion of the object or as a decorative element. The delicate, almost semi-circular ear ornaments (nos. 148-149) of carefully constructed, net-like pattern are perhaps the ultimate expression of this kind of light-pierced work. At the other extreme, on the chests of the well known bird finials, are the spiral decorated open spaces which, because no light can pass through them, become dark spaces instead. The function of these so-called finials (no. 138), which consist of a lid or cap-like element with birds or animals placed to be seen horizontally, has long been problematic. It is thought, as they are quite heavy, cast objects, that they may have been used on top of staffs of some substantial and

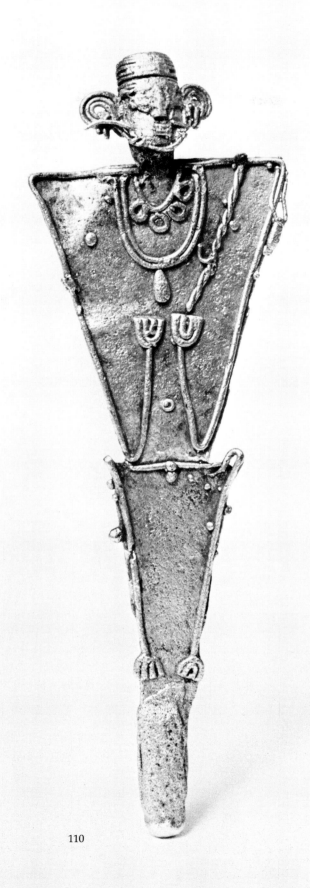

110

important sort, such as staffs of office or rank.

The Tairona were, with the Muiscas (Chibchas), the most developed Indian group in Colombia at the time of the Conquest. Dense populations, efficient agricultural and technological systems, and coherent religions, set them apart from the more local valley chiefdoms which surrounded them. The Tairona lived in the foothills of the Sierra Nevada de Santa Marta in the far north of Colombia, and their goldwork was notably flamboyant. None of the discretion of the so-called Quimbaya gold, nor the subtlety of Muisca gold, is found in Tairona work. The muscular, stubby little human figures with headdresses, bar nose rods, and lip plugs in their lower lip, which appear commonly in the gold of the Tairona area (nos. 166-167), are decidedly pugnacious, their beady eyes peering out from beneath their headdresses at a world they seem all too willing to take on. They are assertive in their very presence, their headdresses enormous, decorated with multiple bird heads, sprays of spirals, circles, dangles. They were virtuoso performers in some ancient life role, and so they were cast by an ancient master craftsman as virtuoso works. Of all the nose-ornament-using cultures of ancient Colombia, none used them more than the Tairona, if the number of extant examples is an indication. In a variety of size and shape, there are among these ornaments those which, to be worn, must have necessitated considerable rearrangement of the interior structure of the wearer's nose. The double bar nose rods of the aforementioned headdressed figures are an example of the nose deforming sort.

The headdressed Tairona figures are, like so many ancient American gold objects, pendants — personal, wearable ornaments. The pendants, the larger pectorals, the arm ornaments, the nose plugs, the ear ornaments, the lime containers, the staff finials, the offering figures, were all of personal scale and for personal use. While the 16th century histories and reports may speak of gold-covered litters (in which personnages of high rank were carried), of wooden idols covered in gold, and of burial mounds marked by great gold bells, these objects are not known today, presumably sought out long ago and destroyed. What is known then, and can be seen now, are those gold pieces which have been found in tombs during the present century when "Indian gold" has begun to have value in its indigenous form. Four centuries after the conquest of the land of El Dorado, ancient gold, when found, was invariably turned into buillion for the world gold market. We should be grateful that since that time there have been those who have begun to see past the glitter of "Indian gold" to the specialness and beauty of its ancient form.

References

BOGOTÁ, EL MUSEO DEL ORO

1971 Bibliography of Pre-Hispanic Gold-work of Colombia. *El Museo del Oro, Estudios*, vol. 1, no. 1, Banco de la República, Bogotá.

1973 *El Dorado*, Edición del Cincuentenario, Banco de la República, 1923-73. Museo del Oro, Banco de la República, Bogotá.

EMMERICH, ANDRÉ

1965 *Sweat of the Sun and Tears of the Moon.* Washington University Press, Seattle.

GROSSMAN, JOEL

1972 An ancient gold worker's tool kit. *Archaeology*, vol. 25, no. 4: 270-75.

1974 Personal communication based on additional radiocarbon information on the Waywaca material.

LOTHROP, SAMUEL KIRLAND

1941 Gold ornaments of Chavin style from Peru. *American Antiquity*, vol. 6, no. 3: 250-62.

1951 Gold artifacts of Chavin style. *American Antiquity*, vol. 16, no. 3: 226-40.

MADRID, EXPOSICIÓN-HISTÓRICO-AMERICANA

[1892] *Catálogo de los objetos que presenta El Gobierno de Colombia a la Exposición Histórico-Americana de Madrid*, text by Ernesto Restrepo Tirado and Isaac Arais. Madrid.

1895 *Report upon the collections exhibited at the Columbian Historical Exposition*, by Daniel G. Brinton. From the report of the Madrid Commission, 1892. Washington, D.C.

PÉREZ DE BARRADAS, JOSÉ

1954 *Orfebreria Prehispanica de Colombia, Estilo Calima*, 2 vol. Talleres Gráficos Jura, Madrid.

1958 *Orbefreria Prehispanica de Colombia, Estilos Tolima y Muisca*, 2 vols. Talleres Gráficos Jura, Madrid.

1966 *Orfebreria Prehispanica de Colombia, Estilos Quimbaya y Otros*, 2 vols. Talleres Gráficos Jura, Madrid.

REICHEL-DOLMATOFF, GERARDO

1965 *Colombia.* Praeger, New York.

ROOT, WILLIAM CAMPBELL

1964 Pre-Columbian metalwork of Colombia and its neighbors. *Essays in Pre-Columbian Art and Archaeology*, pp. 242-57. Harvard University Press, Cambridge.

Muisca raft thought to depict the El Dorado ceremony. Provenance: Pasca, Cundinamarca. (not in exhibition.)

31

Gold Working in Ancient America

WARWICK BRAY
INSTITUTE OF ARCHAEOLOGY
LONDON UNIVERSITY

The Spanish conquest of the Caribbean Islands and mainland South America brought with it a host of adventurers, scholars, and officials, some of whom had a professional concern with metalworking and have left valuable accounts of native technology. Girolamo Benzoni, whose *History of the New World* appeared in 1572, was an Italian silversmith and jeweller, while Gonzalo Fernández de Oviedo was the king's supervisor of smelting operations in Tierra Firme (the old Spanish Main, which included Caribbean Colombia) from 1513 to 1532. One of the earliest descriptions in English occurs in a book which Sir Walter Ralegh sonorously, if optimistically, titled *The Discoverie of the large, rich and bewtiful Empire of Guiana with a relation of the great and Golden Citie of Manoa (which the Spanyards call El Dorado), etc ... performed in the yeare 1595.*

Although badly misled by rumours of a golden city in the interior of Guyana, Ralegh did obtain some practical information from a chieftain of the Epuremei, who lived south of the river Orinoco. This lord told Ralegh that the Indians:

> "put to [the gold] a part of copper, otherwise they coulde not worke it, and that they used a great earthen potte with holes round about it, and when they had mingled the gold and copper together, they fastned canes to the holes, and so with the breath of men they increased the fire till the metall ran, then they cast it into moulds of stone and clay, and so make those plates and Images."

These observations apply to many parts of America, and can serve as a general introduction to aboriginal technology.

Casting

The metal objects described by Ralegh's informant were made of a gold-copper alloy known as *tumbaga* or *guanin gold*. Ralegh himself noted that there was a "triall made of an Image of Copper made in *Guiana*, which helde a third part gold." This analysis confirmed an earlier one made on a specimen which Columbus brought back from the island of Hispañiola; it had contained 18 parts of gold to 16 of silver and 8 of copper. The silver, which is found in much American tumbaga and which can constitute up to 25% of the total weight, was present as an impurity in the gold. It was not added intentionally.

Although Ralegh's Indians maintained that gold could not be cast without the addition of copper, the natives of Panama and Colombia had no trouble casting pure gold as well as gold-rich alloys with exactly the same technology. It is true, however, that tumbaga is easier to cast than any of its constituent metals alone. An alloy of 18% copper with 82% gold melts at 800°C, which is well below the melting points of pure gold (1063°), copper (1083°) or silver (1420°). Laboratory tests have shown that awls, chisels and axes of tumbaga were usually finished by cold hammering, and that the resultant edge is nearly as hard as cold-worked bronze.

Ralegh's description does not make it clear whether the casting moulds were of open or closed type, nor whether the "images" were cast by the lost wax process. Open moulds, usually for the casting of axes or chisels, are fairly common in Ecuador and the central Andes, but have not yet been found in Colombia. Closed, multi-piece moulds are rare in the New World, but this technique was used in the manufacture of one of the best known Colombian objects — an incense burner now displayed with the rest of the *Treasure of the Quimbayas* in the Museo de América, Madrid. The incensario is in the shape of a human head and has a raised seam, inside and out, dividing the vessel vertically into two sections and showing where a little metal ran into the join between the two halves of the mould.

All but the simplest casts were made, with few exceptions, by the lost wax (*cire perdue*) method. To make hollow objects, the craftsman first prepared a core of clay mixed with powdered charcoal, and carved it into the shape of the finished product. He then took purified beeswax mixed with a kind of resin, which acted as a hardening agent, and rolled the compound out into a thin sheet. He laid this over the core and the final incised or appliqué details were added. The wax model was brushed with an emulsion of liquid clay and charcoal dust, and then the whole thing was enveloped in a thick layer of clay. Wooden pegs (chaplets) passed through the wax and held the core in position so that it would not move during the casting process.

The top of the outer clay casing was formed into a little cup-shaped reservoir connected by a channel to the wax model. Vent holes pierced the outer mould at various points, allowing gases to escape and preventing the formation of air pockets which would cause bubbles in the cast metal. The mould was placed with the cup upwards after it had dried slowly in the air. Heated to a high temperature, the wax vapourised leaving a space between the core and the outer casing. While the mould was still hot, molten metal was poured into the reservoir flowing down the connecting channel to take the place of the melted wax. This technique gives an exact copy of even the most delicate wax model and — because the outer casing has to be broken in order to extract the metal — each cast is an original creation. The largest single-piece castings are the Quimbaya flasks, which may weigh two pounds or more. Except for the chaplet holes, which are still visible on several of the larger figures, Quimbaya goldsmiths removed all traces of workmanship. Many of the hollow pieces still retain the original core, and the charcoal content is often high enough to provide a sample for radiocarbon dating.

The Muisca (Chibcha) figurines which were made primarily for votive purposes and were less carefully finished, are the best for studying the technology of casting. Certain Muisca specimens, notably the hollow seated figures, clearly show the pattern of the overlapping strips of wax which were laid over the core. Further technical details can be seen on the flat figurines called *tunjos*, many of which still have black fragments of the clay-and-charcoal covering adhering to their surfaces. A few tunjos are more or less untouched, just as they came from the mould. They were cast head downwards, and still have a button of metal at the foot where the reservoir cup was attached to the mould. Rod-shaped protuberances will show where a little metal flowed into the channels and air vents, and was not cleaned off when the figurine was removed from its casing.

At first glance many Colombian objects appear to have been made by the filigree process in which pieces of coiled or twisted wire are soldered together. Closer examination shows that the technique is in fact "false filigree," cast by the lost wax method. Thin wire-like threads were obtained by squeezing molten wax through a fine nozzle into cold water. These threads were used to build up a wax model, and the entire specimen was then cast in a single operation. False filigree was used to best advantage in the fan-shaped ear ornaments from the Sinú region and in the Muisca tunjos, whose faces, limbs and costumes were modelled from wax threads fixed to a flat plaque of the same material. Hollow objects — in particular bells and models of animals, birds or shells — were made in a similar manner by coiling wax thread round a preshaped core.

Casting tools

Tools used in the melting and casting processes have been found in many parts of Colombia, though rarely in controlled archaeological excavations. The Museo del Oro possesses two unusual stone tables which may perhaps have been used for rolling out wax. Each of these miniature tables has six stumpy feet, and one example is complete with its upper stone shaped like a flattened cylinder. From the Quimbaya zone comes a portable furnace or brazier 29 cm. high. The upper portion is shaped like a bowl with holes in the bottom, and is attached to a hollow pedestal with a tube at the side. This 'earthen potte' shows no traces of fire, but it is suggested that a crucible was placed in the upper half and a charcoal fire lit inside the pedestal, forced draft being created by the attachment of a blowpipe to the spout. A clay tube, suitable for use as a blowpipe, has recently been found at Pasca in Muisca territory.

Travellers' tales and the reminiscences of tomb robbers make it clear that crucibles have been discovered both in cemeteries and at workshop sites. Few complete examples have been preserved, but a grave near Ginebra (on the eastern flank of the Cauca Valley) yielded two fine crucibles — one provided with a spout, the other with a groove below the rim to take a handle made from a bent twig.

The well-known Muisca stone matrices were also part of the caster's equipment. On each facet of these stone blocks are patterns in high relief, depicting the familiar motifs of Muisca goldwork: frogs, fish, human faces, long-beaked birds and abstract patterns. Contrary to popular belief, the matrices were not used for the direct production of repoussé objects in sheet metal but for pressing out the clay and charcoal moulds to be employed in lost wax casting. This technique of mass production was used to make necklaces of identical figures and to make standardized elements which could be assembled in various ways at the wax model stage. The joins from this assembly process are often clearly visible in the cast metal versions.

Hammering and embossing

In his account of the Tamara Indians who lived near the confluence of the Magdalena and César rivers, Oviedo describes hammering and melting:

> "they have their forges, anvils and hammers, which are of
> hard stone: some people say they are of black metal similar to
> emery. The hammers are the size of eggs or somewhat smal-
> ler, and the anvils (which are of very hard stone) are as big as
> a Mallorca cheese. For bellows they use canes, three fingers
> or more in thickness and two palms in length. They have
> delicate steelyards with which they weigh..."

The accuracy of these observations is confirmed by archaeological evidence. Balances have been reported from several looted graves in Quimbaya territory, and the collections of the Museo del Oro include a hammer-and-anvil set which exactly matches Oviedo's description.

19

Hammering was used to stretch and planish the flat parts of certain cast items, but was also an important technique in its own right. Ingots were beaten out into nose-ornaments, plaques, and pendants, or were converted into metal sheet. Pure gold is soft and easy to beat out, but under repeated hammering copper and tumbaga first become springy and difficult to work, then turn brittle. To restore malleability these metals must be annealed, that is replaced in the furnace and brought to red heat, after which they can be hammered again.

With alternate hammering and annealing, metalsmiths were able to produce complex shapes such as the Quimbaya helmets or the Calima breastplates with human faces in high relief. Tool marks show that the sheet metal was cut out with chisels, then pressed into concave moulds of wood or stone, or else hammered and pressed over patterns in high relief. Further decoration was added by embossing from the back and by engraving or chasing on the front of the piece. Complicated objects, like hollow figurines or multi-piece ornaments, were made from separate elements joined by stapling, clinching, soldering, or hammer welding.

Gilding

Many objects which appear to be of pure gold are actually made of tumbaga with a high copper content. A few specimens are actually covered with gold foil, but more frequently in American metallurgy some form of *depletion gilding* was used. This produces a yellow surface on an object containing gold as one of its constituents. The alloy is treated chemically to remove the base metals from the surface and to leave the surface gold untouched. The result is a surface film of relatively pure gold which completely conceals the base metal tumbaga core. Two techniques were employed to achieve this in prehistoric America. In Tierra Firme all the surviving accounts refer to a *mise en couleur* process employing plant juice. Oviedo commented that the Indians of the mainland used a special herb to gild base gold, and that knowledge of the technique (which they refused to explain to him) would make the fortune of any European goldsmith. Francisco López de Gómara reports a similar process in the

Sinú and Santa Marta regions of Caribbean Colombia:

> "They gild with a certain plant which they crush and squeeze out: they rub the copper [i.e. tumbaga] with it and put it in the fire. The more of the herb they give it the better colour it takes on, and it is so fine that it deceived many Spaniards at first."

The active substance may have been oxalic acid, for Indian goldsmiths in Ecuador still clean jewellery by heating the objects in a copper pot containing a mixture of salt, water, and macerated plants of the Oxalis family.

The second method of depletion gilding, *superficial parting*, relies on acid minerals rather than organic substances. Bernardino de Sahagún records that the Aztecs used a substance known as 'gold medicine' which looked like a mixture of yellow earth and salt. Probably his 'gold medicine' was a corrosive mineral (perhaps one of the hydrated ferric sulphates, which are common in nature), and Heather Lechtman of the Massachusetts Institute of Technology has successfully replicated the process in the laboratory. It seems likely that both *mise en couleur* and superficial parting were known to the ancient Colombians.

Workshop sites

Most of our information on goldworking technology has come from the examination of the finished products. To get a more complete picture of aboriginal metallurgy, laboratory analysis must be complemented by the scientific excavation of workshops and smelting sites of the kind described in early Spanish chronicles. On these sites we can expect to find the waste materials and by-products which give essential technical information but were not thought worthy of burial in tombs: the slags, crushers, furnaces, broken crucibles, moulds, and the clay casings from lost wax casting. Workshop sites undoubtedly exist; there are many tantalizing reports of such discoveries made before the days of scientific archaeology.

Some of our most detailed information on workshop practices comes from Esmeraldas, in coastal Ecuador just south of the Colombian frontier. During Prehispanic times the Department of Esmeraldas and the Tumaco region of Colombia were a single cultural province, sharing the same pottery, figurines, and metal technology. Placer mining at La Tolita and other localities has unearthed thousands of small objects washed out from destroyed or undiscovered sites, and this material includes numerous unfinished and partially worked objects which allow the processes of manufacture to be studied.

Among the finds were gold nuggets up to 30 grams in weight.

Metallurgical examination proved that these were in fact ingots of melted gold. None showed signs of having been in a crucible, but several bore the imprint of wood grain, suggesting that small pieces of metal had been fused on a piece of charcoal with the aid of a blowpipe. Some of the nuggets proved to be lumps of alloy, and one imperfectly fused example still had a piece of copper encased in the gold. Other specimens demonstrated that scrap was remelted, and there were also pieces of foil hammered together ito little packages ready for melting. The fused metal was then hammered, with occasional heating, into ingots or sheets.

The metallurgy of platinum

Besides the usual copper, gold, and tumbaga, the jewellers of the Pacific coast of South America worked lead and — more remarkably — platinum. Platinum was not recognized as a separate metal in Europe until 1750. Metallic platinum occurs as small grains in the gold-bearing gravels of the rivers which drain towards the Pacific through Esmeraldas, Nariño, and the Colombian Chocó. Since it is found as specks of pure metal, unalloyed with gold, it can easily be separated out by washing and hand sorting, but because of its high melting point (1775°C) it could not be liquefied with the equipment available to Indian metalsmiths. Casting of pure platinum was therefore impossible, but analysis of Ecuadorean ornaments shows that native jewelers sidestepped this problem by sintering the platinum with gold. The grains of platinum were mixed with a little gold dust, and the mixture was heated on a bed of charcoal. Under this treatment the gold melts and flows, binding the platinum granules together. Hammering further consolidates the mixture and, in addition, a little of each metal flows into the other to form a homogeneous mass. Even though the platinum has never melted, the resultant compound can be forged or cast much like a true alloy.

Chemical analysis of "platinum" jewellery from La Tolita shows that the actual platinum content usually varies between 26% and 76%. The addition of platinum to gold has the effect of hardening and bleaching the compound. In concentrations as low as 4% the colour change is noticeable, and at 13% the metal becomes a greyish yellow. It was thus important to keep platinum out of jewellery when a rich yellow was the desired colour. The analysis of "gold" objects from Tolita indicated less than 2% platinum. At this level, the platinum is clearly an accidental impurity resulting from poor sorting at the panning stage.

Platinum objects are not very common, but in Colombian territory Sigvald Linné discovered a hammered nose-ornament in a grave at Cupica in the northern Chocó, and the Museo del Oro owns a few specimens said to come from sites in the Andes, where they were evidently trade pieces.

The Organization of the Metal Trade

WARWICK BRAY
INSTITUTE OF ARCHAEOLOGY
LONDON UNIVERSITY

One of the most difficult things to assess by archaeological means is the number of people involved in metallurgical activities and the quantity of artifacts and raw metal they produced in the ancient New World. Documentary sources must be relied upon for this information, and for Colombia several 16th century Spanish eyewitness descriptions of native Indian culture — before it disintegrated under the impact of European conquest — fortunately exist.

The Spanish settlements on the Gulf of Urabá were the ports of entry for expeditions into Colombia. In 1536-37 Francisco César defeated the tribes of the upper Sinú and plundered their graves; he obtained 20,000 pesos of gold (183 lbs.) from a single tomb. In 1538, Juan de Vadillo followed, continuing as far as the highlands of Antioquia. In Vadillo's entourage was the young Pedro Cieza de León who wrote a classic account of Antioquia and the Quimbaya tribes of the Cauca Valley. The first of three separate expeditions to converge on Bogotá, the capital of the principal Muisca chiefdom, arrived in 1537, led by Gonzalo Jiménez de Quesada, who ascended the Rio Magdalena from the port of Santa Marta. The original Jiménez de Quesada diaries and letters were lost, but extracts from them were incorporated in the works of Oviedo y Valdés and Juan de Castellanos.

Mining and metal extraction

The Spanish accounts tell of the Indian exploitation of alluvial gold, from the sands and gravels of river beds, and of the mining the gold, when it occurred as thin veins of metal in hard rock. Both processes required only the simplest tools.

Placer mining was usually a dry season activity. Workmen broke up the overburden with fire-hardened digging sticks and removed the gravel in scoops. Dams of stone or wood were built when necessary, to prevent the washing down of debris and to provide a controlled water supply. The gravel was sluiced and stirred, then the gold-bearing residue was hand washed in wooden trays. Oviedo, who observed miners at work on the north coast, remarked that they worked in teams: two men to dig and break up the earth, and two to carry it in trays to the nearest stream where it was panned by groups of women. By these rudimentary methods a 20 lb. load of gravel was processed in less than 10 minutes.

Deep mines for extracting vein gold were also mentioned by the Spanish chroniclers, but no Colombian site of this kind has been scientifically excavated. One of the best descriptions dates from the 1880's, when the English engineer R. B. White visited the Prehispanic and early colonial mines of Los Remedios, in Antioquia. This province was among the richest gold-producing areas of the New World, and White discovered an extensive system of shafts, spaced at intervals of four or five yards. Each mine was a simple pit no more than 3 feet wide, excavated down to the gold-bearing quartz lodes. There was no attempt at shoring, nor were ventilation systems or side galleries present. The deepest vertical shafts were 60 to 80 feet deep and had steps cut in the sides. The sloping shafts, inclined at about 30°, were up to 60 yards long, and so narrow that a man could not turn around in them. The miners must have backed out, dragging their loads behind them. At the surface the excavated material was sorted, broken up, and washed to extract the gold.

In Prehispanic times, as at present, small-scale mining may have been a part time occupation. Some localities, however, were inhabited by specialist communities of miners and smiths. The most famous gold-extraction site in Colombia was Buriticá in northern Antioquia, visited by Juan de Vadillo in 1538 and by Jorge Robledo in 1541. The exact location of the pre-Spanish mining and workshop site has never been rediscovered, but from descriptions published by members of Vadillo's expedition it is evident that Buriticá was a true industrial centre, engaged in exploiting both alluvial and vein gold. The mines were exceptionally rich. Oviedo reports that Vadillo had some of the earth gathered up "and from a quantity sufficient to fill an ordinary shield obtained granules of gold to the value of a ducat [1/10 oz.]."

The houses at Buriticá were all occupied by miners, and some of the deep mines were owned by private individuals. Buriticá itself was a fortified town or village on a hilltop, and references to other sites with furnaces and melting equipment suggest that it was the capital of a mining region. It was not an egalitarian community of workmen, for the chronicles mention both noblemen and slaves. Pedro Simón records the gruesome detail that the lords killed slaves to provide fat for the lamps used in the mine shafts, and then sold off the flesh for food.

The gold was melted down on the spot in crucibles and was

weighed out with balances. Spanish accounts do not distinguish clearly between the melting of bulk metal and melting for the purpose of casting gold ornaments, but the general impression is that the miners exported both finished pieces and raw metal to be worked elsewhere. Some of this surplus was carried southwards to the Quimbayas, and a little was traded to Muisca territory. Most of it, however, made its way to Dabeiba and from there to the Sinú region and the Caribbean coast.

Trade

Dabeiba is an interesting phenomenon: a community of specialist jewellers. Except for a little alluvial gold, it had no metal supplies of its own, but was strategically situated on the trade route which linked the mining centre of Buriticá to the markets in the Sinú and the Gulf of Urabá. In a letter written to the Spanish king in 1513, Nuñez de Balboa remarked that the ruler of Dabeiba was said to have a hundred men engaged in full time gold working, and that the gold was stored in baskets so heavy that a man could barely lift one onto his back. Balboa also observed that "from the house of this lord comes all the gold which reaches the Gulf [of Urabá], all that the chiefs of these regions possess."

Cieza de León noted that professional merchants from the Sinú controlled trade to the interior, and that there were properly regulated markets where they met to barter lowland products for highland gold. In exchange for gold, both worked and unworked, the Sinú merchants offered slaves, fish, salt, cotton cloth, live peccaries, and gold ornaments made in their own workshops. Vadillo, who personally visited the site, commented that Dabeiba goldsmiths made jewellery of the type found in the Sinú and the Gulf of Urabá. This is confirmed by archaeological specimens in pure Sinú style discovered along the route from the coast to the mountainous region of north Antioquia.

The quantity of gold which passed along this route must have been enormous, for the Sinú was the greatest centre for tomb-robbing during the early years of the Conquest. Vadillo's own testament gives some idea of the profits to be won from *guaqueria*:

> "Since the time when it was first occupied and the office of Treasurer was created, that is from 15 January 1533 to 11 December 1534, this Province has yielded 12,126 pesos and 4 tomines of fine gold [about 110 lbs.] and 24 kg. [53 lbs.] of base gold. From December 1534 to 13 July 1537, the sum is 247 kg. [545 lbs.] of fine gold and more than 80 kg. [176 lbs.] of base gold."

By 1537 the amount of loot was so great that the Spanish crown began to fear for its own share, and passed an edict forbidding Vadillo to open graves except in the presence of the King's Overseer.

Another important trade route linked the Tairona peoples of the Sierra Nevada de Santa Marta and the Atlantic coast with the Muisca kingdoms of the Andean plateau, passing by way of the Magdalena Valley, where gold and copper sources had been exploited since early times. This commerce was the basis of Muisca metallurgy, for there were no sources of gold in the Muisca homeland. Copper was available at Moniquirá, and Gachalá, but all gold had to be imported from the tribes of the middle Magdalena Valley. In exchange the highlanders offered cotton cloth, painted mantles, emeralds, and — most important of all — salt from Nemocón and Zipaquirá.

Jiménez de Quesada has left a graphic description of the salt trade as he observed it in March 1537:

> "As we gradually ascended the Río Magdalene we noticed that all the salt which the Indians ate reached them by means of exchanges, and that it came from the sea and from the coasts of Santa Marta. It was bartered in granular form for more than 70 leagues from the mouth of the river. By the time it had reached this point, so little remained that it was very dear, and only the rich could afford to eat it. Poor people made their salt from human urine and from the powdered ashes of plants. After passing La Tora [modern Barranca Bermeja] we came across another salt, not in grains like the other but in solid loaves, and as we journeyed upstream this salt became cheaper and cheaper among the Indians. For this reason, and because of the difference between the two kinds of salt, we concluded that the granular salt was traded up-river and that the salt loaves came from the opposite direction and were traded downstream."

The men from the Magdalena Valley brought gold from their mines and also participated in the shell trade. Large conch shells (sometimes covered in gold leaf) were used as trumpets, and the smaller shells were converted into beads and pendants. Padre Simon reports that the Muiscas "procured these from the coast, from which they arrived, passing from hand to hand, at very high prices." If this is to be believed, it seems that merchants did not make the entire trip of nearly 400 miles, but that objects were traded from one group of middle men to another all along the route.

Certain towns were market centres. One such was Pasca, at the southwest corner of Muisca territory on the way to the Río Magdalena; another was Vélez, just outside the northwestern frontier and close to the

44

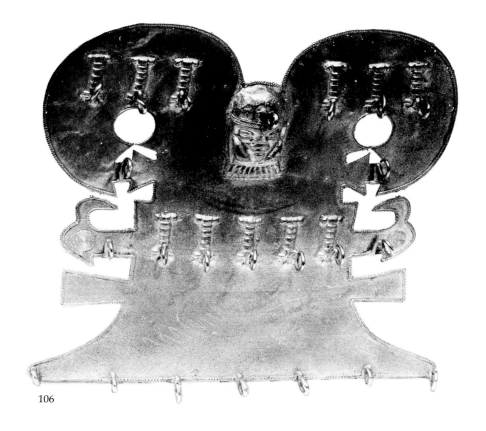

106

headwaters of the rivers Carare and Opón. At Vélez a market was held every eight days, and the town was a centre for the distribution of gold, cotton, cloth, pottery, and coca.

Several colonial authors insist that Muisca traders used 'money' in the form of small *tejuelos* (round, mould-made buttons of cast gold) whose value depended on size, measured against the finger joints or by means of a cotton thread. The conquistadors discovered several hoards of these tejuelos, and a few examples are preserved in museum collections. These archaeological specimens have no consistent pattern of weight or size. Some of them seem to be little ingots of melted gold; others are buttons of waste metal left in the reservoir after casting by the lost wax process. No doubt the tejuelos were bartered like any other commodity, but there is no evidence that they ever served as a true coinage.

There is archaeological proof that Spanish accounts of Muisca trade are not exaggerated. The salt and cloth have left little trace, but in the collection of the Museo del Oro are some Tairona breastplates which show strong stylistic influence from Muisca goldwork. Conch shells have been found at various Muisca sites, and shell beads are abundant wherever archaeologists have investigated cemeteries in the Eastern Cordillera. In the opposite direction, Colombian emeralds travelled as far north as Coclé in Panama.

The trade networks described in Spanish chronicles are those of the 16th century, but the general pattern is of great antiquity. Distribution maps indicate that metal objects (which are both portable and valuable) were carried long distances from their places of origin. Not only is the same technology found over a wide area, but stylistic similarities show that there was constant interchange of ideas and products between the different regions of Colombia. This trade is as old as metallurgy itself.

Maps do not in themselves tell us how or why these exchanges took place. Trade is only one of several possible mechanisms of distribution. Others are pillage, tribute, or pilgrimmage to such holy sites as the lagoon of Guatavita or the cenote at Chicén Itzá in the Maya country of Yucatan. All these activities are recorded in early historical sources.

Another problem concerns the metalsmiths themselves. Where the miner is tied to his ore and his metal deposits, the smith is a free agent; his economic ties are with his patrons and customers, his equipment is portable, and he can work wherever there is a market for his skills. He can make objects in various styles, can pass on technical tricks as well as finished trinkets — and he is virtually unrecognizable by archaeological means.

The only information about the status of the metalsmith comes, yet again, from documentary sources. Juan de Castellanos, resident at Tunja in the 1560's, remarked that the Muisca goldsmiths of Guatavita were highly esteemed specialists in Prehispanic times, travelling throughout the neighbouring provinces and earning a living by their skills in metalworking. He goes on to say that the ruler of the town insisted that anyone who employed a Guatavita smith must send two of his own vassals to work in Guatavita for the duration of the contract. This policy eventually caused the ruler's downfall. Guatavita became full of foreigners, most of whom owed allegiance to the rival kingdom of Bogotá, and on receipt of a signal these infiltrators rose up, massacred the chief, and delivered his town to the enemy. Castellanos is not a very trustworthy source but, true or false, the tale illustrates popular belief in the high status and economic importance of goldsmiths in the Muisca chiefdoms.

Foreign trade

Trade, looting, and pilgrimage can account for the spread of manufactured articles over a wide area, but the transmission of a complex technology like metalworking involves the actual movement of travelling smiths and specialists.

Although the details have still to be worked out, the overall development of New World metallurgy is clear. All sources of evidence confirm that metal technology spread from south to north. In Peru the first objects of hammered gold are dated around 2000 B.C., after which there was a long period of purely local development, with new techniques entering the repertoire from time to time. By contrast, metallurgy appeared suddenly in Mexico sometime between A.D. 700 and 900. There was no period of experimentation: the technology was fully developed from the start. The only reasonable explanation is that knowledge of metallurgy was introduced into Mexico from some point further south, and it is difficult to imagine how this could have been done by traders alone, without the intervention of at least a few itinerant smiths.

The Colombian-Isthmian region lies midway between the Andes and Mexico, and it played a vital role in this transmission. Colombia, Panama and Costa Rica formed a single metallurgical province, characterized by a preference for lost wax casting and by the use of gold-copper alloys, depletion gilding and false filigree.

The regional styles of this province were closely related, and the links between Quimbaya goldwork and the Panamanian styles of Coclé and Veraguas were particularly close. Not only are there many similarities of form (for example, embossed helmets and cast figurines of human beings, animals, and eagles), but actual trade pieces were carried in both directions. Panamanian gold objects have been found as far south as Armenia in the Quindío, and Quimbaya figurines — or close copies — have been unearthed in graves at Las Mercedes and other sites in the Linea Vieja district of north-east Costa Rica, and northwards to Tazumal in El Salvador. The most popular Colombian exports were the so-called 'Darien' pendants in the shape of stylized human figures wearing head-dresses with mushroom-like appendages. Probably manufactured somewhere in Quimbaya territory, these pendants have been found at Venado Beach and Parita in Panama, and at La Fortuna in the Linea Vieja region of Costa Rica.

In time, as well as in space, the Colombian-Isthmian metal industries fall midway between those of Peru and Mexico. On present evidence, metallurgy reached Colombia before the time of Christ, and Panama by A.D. 300-500 at latest, although in these countries the bulk of the goldwork was made between A.D. 500 and the Spanish conquest. The oldest archaeological specimen from Mesoamerica is a claw-shaped pendant of tumbaga from a Maya tomb at Altun Ha (Belize). It was probably made in Coclé sometime before A.D. 500, but the arrival of such isolated trade pieces, divorced from the accompanying technology, did not lead to the establishment of local metal industries in Mexico or Maya territory.

This happened some two or three centuries later, when (we must assume), Isthmian goldsmiths first began to travel the northern routes. After about A.D. 800, metal objects became more common in Mesoamerica and included ornaments in local styles as well as trade items. Some of these locally made objects still show the influence of their foreign prototypes. The most common models were the gold pendants in the shape of frogs with flattened rectangular feet, manufactured in the Veraguas and Chiriquí regions of Panama. These were copied in highland Guatemala and Oaxaca and were one of the formative influences on Mixtec goldwork.

With the introduction of the new technology into Mexico, the local smiths quickly freed themselves from foreign influences and evolved their own independent styles of metalworking. In Honduras, El Salvador, and the Maya zone, the trade links with the Isthmus remained important up to the Spanish conquest — so much so that two thirds of the gold thrown into the Sacred Well at Chichén Itzá, Yucatan, consisted of Panamanian bells and figurines. With the scale of this commerce in mind, it is not so surprising that the cenote treasure also included two 'Darien' pendants brought all the way from Colombia.

Perhaps the traders came by sea, like the group which Columbus met near the Bay Islands of Honduras in the year 1502. In the words of Bartolomé de las Casas:

"a canoe full of Indians arrived, as long as a galley and 8 feet broad... In the middle of the canoe they had an awning made of palm matting, which they call *petates* in New Spain. Inside, under this, were their women, children, belongings and goods, so that neither sea water nor rain could wet anything. The goods which they brought were many cotton blankets of gay colours and designs, sleeveless shirts with coloured patterns, and some of the sashes with which they cover their private parts. They also had wooden swords with flint blades glued to the edges, and small copper hatchets to cut wood, and some bells and medallions, and crucibles to melt the copper. Seeing the ships of the Christians, they did not dare defend themselves, but were taken in their canoe to the Admiral's Ship."

This eyewitness description not only proves the existence of travelling metalsmiths, but also gives a rare glimpse of the human reality behind the archaeological evidence.

References

ARANGO C., LUIS

1924 *Recuerdos de la Guaquería en el Quindío.* Editorial Cremos, Bogotá.

ARSANDAUX, H. AND RIVET, PAUL

1923 L'Orfèvrerie du Chiriquí et de Colombie. *Journal de la Société des Américanistes de Paris,* N.S. vol. 15: 169-82.

BALSER, CARLOS

1968 Metal and Jade in Lower Central America. *Actas y Memorias, 37 Congreso Internacional de Americanistas,* vol. 4: 57-63. Librart, Buenos Aires.

BARBA, ALVARO ALONZO

1923 *El Arte de los Metales,* ed. R. E. Douglass and E. P. Mathewson. J. Wiley and Sons, New York.

BENZONI, GIROLAMO

1857 *History of the New World,* ed. W. H. Smyth. The Hakluyt Society, London.

BERGSOE, PAUL

1937 The Metallurgy and Technology of Gold and Platinum among the Pre-Columbian Indians. *Ingeniørvidenskabelige Skrifter,* No. A.44. Copenhagen.

1938 The Gilding Process and the Metallurgy of Copper and Lead among the Pre-Columbian Indians. *Ingeniørvidenskabelige Skrifter,* No. A.46. Copenhagen.

BIESE, LEO P.

1967 The Gold of Parita. *Archaeology,* vol. 20, no. 3: 202-8.

BOLIAN, CHARLES E.

1973 Seriation of Darien Style Anthropomorphic Figurines. In Donald W. Lathrap and Jody Douglas (eds.), *Variation in Anthropology:* 213-32. Illinois Archaeological Survey, Urbana.

BRAY, WARWICK

1972 Ancient American Metal-Smiths. *Proceedings of the Royal Anthropological Institute of Great Britain and Ireland for 1971:* 25-43.

BRIGHT, ALEC

1972 A goldsmith's blowpipe from Colombia. *Man,* vol. 7, no.2: 311-3.

BRUHNS, KAREN OLSEN

1970 A Quimbaya Gold Furnace? *American Antiquity,* vol. 35, no. 2: 202-3.

1972 Two Prehispanic Cire Perdue Casting Moulds from Colombia. *Man,* vol. 7, no. 2: 308-11.

1972 The Methods of Guaquería: Illicit Tomb Looting in Colombia. *Archaeology,* vol. 25, no. 2: 240-43.

CASO, ALFONSO

1965 Lapidary Work, Goldwork and Copperwork from Oaxaca. In R. Wauchope (gen. ed), *Handbook of Middle American Indians,* vol. 3, part 2: 896-930. University of Texas Press, Austin.

CASTELLANOS, JUAN DE

1955 *Elegías de Varones Ilustres de Indias, Part 4: Historia del Neuvo Reino de Granada.* Vol. 12 of Obras de Juan de Castellanos, Edicion de la Presidencia de Colombia. Editorial ABC, Bogotá.

CIEZA DE LEÓN, PEDRO DE

1864 *The Travels of Pedro de Cieza de Léon, A.D. 1532-50, Contained in the First Part of his Chronicle of Peru,* trans. Clements R. Markham. The Hakluyt Society, London.

DUQUE GÓMEZ, LUIS

1958 Notas Históricas sobre la Orfebrería Indígena en Colombia. In *Homenaje al Profesor Paul Rivet:* 271-335. Academia Colombiana de Historia, Editorial ABC, Bogotá.

EASBY, DUDLEY T.

1956 Sahagun Reviviscit in the Gold Collections of the University Museum. *University Museum Bulletin* (Philadelphia), vol. 20, no. 3: 3-15.

1965 Pre-Hispanic Metallurgy and Metalworking in the New World. *Proceedings of the American Philosophical Society,* vol. 109, no. 2: 89-98.

1966 Early Metallurgy in the New World. *Scientific American,* vol. 214, no. 4: 73-81.

EMMERICH, ANDRÉ

1965 *Sweat of the Sun and Tears of the Moon.* Washington University Press, Seattle.

1967 *Gods and Men in Pre-Columbian Art.* André Emmerich Inc., New York.

FRIEDE, JUAN

1951 Breves Informaciones sobre la Metalurgía de los Indios de Santa Marta segun Documentos Encontrados en al Archivo de Indias, Sevilla. *Journal de la Société des Américanistes de Paris,* N.S. vol. 40: 197-202.

GONZÁLEZ GUZMÁN, RAÚL

1971 Informe sobre excavaciones arqueológicas realizadas en El Cafetal, Distrito de Tonosi, Provincia de Los Santos, Panama. *Actas del II Symposium Nacional de Antropologia, Arqueologia y Etnohistoria de Panama:* 143-74. Universidad de Panama.

HULTREN, AXEL

1931 The hardness of Colombian tools made from copper-gold-silver alloys. *Comparative Ethnological Studies,* vol.9: 108-12.

LAS CASAS, BARTOLOMÉ DE

1951 *Historia de las Indias.* Edit. Millares Carlo, Mexico.

LECHTMAN, HEATHER N.

1971 Ancient Methods of Gilding Silver: Examples from the Old and New Worlds. In Robert H. Brill (ed.) *Science and Archaeology:* 2-30. Massachusetts Institute of Technology.

1973 The Gilding of Metals in Pre-Columbian Peru. In William J. Young (ed.) *Application of Science in Examination of Works of Art:* 38-52. Museum of Fine Arts, Boston.

1973 A Tumbaga Object from the High Andes of Venezuela. *American Antiquity,* vol. 38, no.4: 473-482.

LINNÉ, SIGVALD

1929 *Darien in the Past: the archaeology of eastern Panama and northwestern Colombia.* Elanders Boktryckeri Aktiebolag. Gothenburg.

115

LONG, STANLEY

1964 Cire Perdue Copper Casting in Pre-Columbian Mexico: An Experimental Approach. *American Antiquity*, vol. 30, no. 2: 189-92.

LÓPEZ DE GOMARA, FRANCISCO

1852 Hispania victrix: Primera y segunda parte de la historia general de las Indias. In E. de Vedia (ed.) *Historiadores primitivos de Indias*, vol. 1: 155-455. Biblioteca de Autores Espanoles, vol. 22. Madrid.

LOTHROP, SAMUEL KIRKLAND

1937 Coclé: An Archaeological Study of Central Panama, Part 1. *Memoirs of the Peabody Museum of Archaeology & Ethnology*, vol. 7. Cambridge.

1952 Metals from the Cenote of Sacrifice, Chichen Itza, Yucatan. *Memoirs of the Peabody Museum of Archaeology & Ethnology*, vol. 10, no. 2. Cambridge.

LOTHROP, S. K. AND BERGSØE, PAUL

1960 Aboriginal Gilding in Panama. *American Antiquity*, vol. 26, no. 1: 106-8.

McGIMSEY, CHARLES R.

1968 A Provisional Dichotomization of Regional Styles in Panamanian Goldwork. *Actas y Memorias, 37 Congreso Internacional de Americanistas*, vol. 4: 45-55. Librart, Buenos Aires.

NISSER, PEDRO

1834 *Sketch of the Different Mining and Mechanical Operations Employed in Some South American Goldworks, as well ancient as modern.* Stockholm.

NORDENSKIÖLD, ERLAND

1931 Ancient Colombian tools of gold alloy. *Comparative Ethnographical Studies*, vol. 9: 101-7.

OVIEDO Y VALDÉS, GONZALO FERNÁNDEZ DE

1959 *Historia general y natural de las Indias, islas y tierra-firme del mar oceano*, 5 vols. Biblioteca de Autores Espanoles. Editorial Atlas, Madrid.

PATTERSON, CLAIR C.

1971 Native Copper, Silver and Gold Accessible to Early Metallurgists. *American Antiquity*, vol. 36, no. 3: 286-321.

PENDERGAST, DAVID M.

1970 Tumbaga Object from the Early Classic Period, Found at Altun Ha, British Honduras (Belize). *Science*, vol. 168: 116-8.

PÉREZ DE BARRADAS, JOSÉ

1950-51 *Los Muiscas antes de la Conquista*, 2 vol. Consejo Superior de Investigaciones Cientificas, Instituto Bernardino de Sahagún, Madrid.

1954 *Orfebrería Prehispánica de Colombia, Estilo Calima*, 2 vols. Talleres Graficos "Jura," Madrid.

1955 *Les Indiens de l'Eldorado; Étude historique et ethnographique des Muiscas de Colombie.* Payot, Paris.

1958 *Orfebrería Prehispánica de Colombia, Estilos Tolima y Muisca*, 2 vols. Talleres Graficos "Jura," Madrid.

1966 *Orfebrería Prehispánica de Colombia, Estilos Quimbaya y Otros*, 2 vols. Talleres Graficos "Jura," Madrid.

RALEGH, SIR WALTER

1848 *The discovery of the large, rich and beautiful empire of Guiana*, ed. R. H. Schomburgk. The Hakluyt Society, London.

REICHEL-DOLMATOFF, GERARDO

1958 Notas sobre la Metalurgia Prehistorica en el Litoral Caribe de Colombia. In *Homenaje al Profesor Paul Rivet*: 69-94. Academia Colombiana de Historia, Editorial ABC. Bogotá.

REICHLEN, HENRY

1942 Contribution à l'Étude de la Métallurgie Précolombienne de la Province d'Esmeraldas (Equateur). *Journal de la Société des Américanistes de Paris.* N.S., vol. 34: 201-28.

RESTREPO, VICENTE

1952 *Estudio sobre las Minas de Oro y Plata de Colombia.* Banco de la Republica, Archivo de la Economia Nacional, Nacional, Bogota.

RIVET, PAUL

1921 Note Complémentaire sur la Métallurgie Sud-Américaine. *Journal de la*

Société des Américanistes de Paris, N.S., vol. 13: 233-8.

1923 L'Orfèvrerie Précolombienne des Antilles, des Guyanes et du Vénézuela, dans ses rapports avec l'orfèvrerie et la métallurgie des autres regions américaines. *Journal de la Société des Américanistes de Paris*, N.S. vol. 15: 183-213.

1924 L'Orfèvrerie Colombienne: Technique, Aire de Dispersion, Origine. *Proceedings of the 21st International Congress of Americanists*, vol. 1: 15-28. The Hague.

1943 Metalurgia del Platino en la America Precolombina. *Revista del Instituto Etnológico Nacional*, vol. 1: 39-45.

RIVET, PAUL AND ARSANDAUX, H.

1946 La métallurgie en Amérique précolombienne. *Travaux et Mémoires de l'Institut d'Ethnologie*, no. 39. Musée de l'Homme, Paris.

ROOT, WILLIAM CAMPBELL

1949 Metallurgy. In J. H. Steward (ed.) *Handbook of South American Indians*, vol. 5: 205-225. Bulletin 143 of the Smithsonian Institution Bureau of American Ethnology, Washington.

1964 Pre-Columbian Metalwork of Colombia and its Neighbors. In S. K. Lothrop (ed.) *Essays in Pre-Columbian Art and Archaeology*: 242-57. Harvard University Press, Cambridge.

SAHAGÚN, BERNARDINO DE

1959 Book 9 of the General History of the Things of New Spain: Florentine Codex, trans. Arthur J. O. Anderson & Charles E. Dibble. *Monographs of the School of American Research*, No. 14, Part 10. Santa Fe.

SIMÓN, PEDRO

1953 *Noticias Historiales de las Conquistas de Tierra Firme en las Indias Occidentales*. Vol. 2. Biblioteca de Autores Colombianos, Editorial Kelly, Bogota.

STONE, DORIS AND BALSER, CARLOS

1965 Incised Slate Discs from the Atlantic Watershed of Costa Rica. *American Antiquity*, vol. 30, no. 3: 310-29.

1967 *Aboriginal Metalwork in lower Central America*. Editorial Antonio Lehmann, San Jose, Costa Rica.

TRIMBORN, HERMANN

1943 Tres Estudios para la Etnografía y Arqueología de Colombia: Los Reinos de Guaca y Nore. *Revista de Indias*, Año 4, No. 11: 43-91; No. 12: 331-47; No. 13: 441-56; No. 14: 629-81.

1944 Tres Estudios para la Etnografía y Arqueología de Colombia: Las Minas de Buriticá. *Revista de Indias*, Año 5, No. 15: 27-39; No. 16: 199-226.

1949 *Señorío y Barbarie en el valle del Cauca.* Instituto Gonzalo Fernandez de Oviedo, Consejo Superior de Investigaciones Cientificas, Madrid.

WASSEN, HENRY

1955 Algunos datos del comercio precolombino en Colombia. *Revista Colombiana de Antropologia*, vol. 4: 87-109.

WEAVER, MURIEL PORTER

1972 *The Aztecs, Maya, and Their Predecessors: Archaeology of Mesoamerica*. Seminar Press, New York & London.

WHITE, ROBERT B.

1884 Notes on the Aboriginal Races of the North-Western Provinces of South America. *Journal of the Anthropological Institute of Great Britain and Ireland*, vol. 13: 240-58.

Note: References here listed cover both "Goldworking in Ancient America" and "The Organization of the Metal Trade."

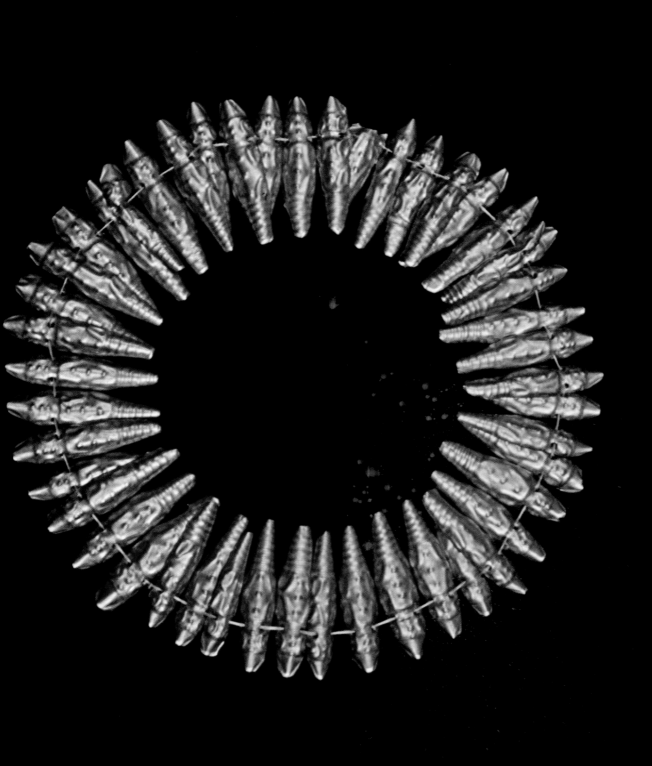

El Museo del Oro, Bogotá

History of El Museo del Oro, Bogotá

El Museo del Oro of the Bank of the Republic was founded in 1939 through the cooperative efforts of Julio Caro and Dr. Luis Angel Arango, then Manager and Assistant Manager of the bank, and the Bank's Board of Directors. Their purpose was to collect and preserve examples of Prehispanic metalwork from Colombia which were, in the main, unappreciated at the time. Despite the archeological importance of these objects, they were valued only for their gold content and were often melted down by the foundries. The collection of El Museo del Oro was begun with purchases from individuals or from treasure hunters and by the acquisition of already extant private collections.

The education of the general public is one of the primary objectives of El Museo del Oro. The architectural design of the building and the arrangement of the exhibitions lead the visitor first through halls which contain general information concerning the various cultural and geographical environments of the metal-working peoples of Colombia. Then, in a specially guarded gallery, the Museum displays most of its collection of gold objects. The Museum presently owns almost 20,000 pieces.

Visitors to the Museum may enjoy daily films and guided tours in both Spanish and English. Moreover, guided tours in other languages are available for special visitors and for schools and other similar organizations. The latter are charged no admission. In preparation for their visit, the Museum offers these groups introductory lectures at their own institutions. The Museum has approximately 180,000 visitors a year and to keep the exhibitions up-to-date and to display new material to regular visitors, the Museum periodically changes its exhibits and installs temporary ones. The temporary exhibits study in detail subjects that are related to the Museum's own collection and purposes. A new exhibit begins early each year. In 1973 an exhibit entitled "The Muiscas from the Land of 'El Dorado' " was presented. "Gold in Colombian History" will be on view during 1974.

The Museum's work is not confined to its center in Bogotá as part of the collection goes on tour regularly both within Colombia and abroad. In the last two years the Museum has sent exhibitions to the Colombian cities of Manizales, Popayan, and Pasto. A show of two hundred pieces has recently visited Madrid, Seville, Rome, Hamburg, Geneva, Brussels, Bucharest, and Paris. Within the next few months exhibitions organized by the Museum will be seen in Tokyo, Monaco, and New York.

For those with a scholarly interest in Precolumbian archeology, the Museum provides research carrels, a specialized library of 4,000 volumes, a card catalogue to the collection, photographs and tapes pertinent to archeological and ethnographic material, and workrooms where the artifacts are studied and restored. The student also has access to the document archives of the Research Department, which is responsible for the archeological studies related to the Museum's collection. Finally, in the Department of Museography, the serious student can investigate research methods as well as procedures for mounting and maintaining both temporary and permanent exhibits.

Introduction to the collections of El Museo del Oro

I During the period of Conquest, the Spaniards made an intensive search for "The Golden Lands." Fantastic legends located golden treasures in different regions of the New World: in the Seven Cities of Cibola in North America, in Pirú (modern Peru), and Manoa (probably Venezuela in South America.) The most famous of these legends is the one that tells of "El Dorado" (The Golden One) and the ceremony which was supposedly held at Lake Guatavita in Colombia. Situated some ten kilometers from the village of Guatavita and approximately 3,199 meters above sea level, the lake measures four kilometers in circumference, and is forty meters deep.

This was where the ritual, briefly described by Fr. Pedro Simón, was believed to take place:

"...using two lines long enough to stretch from one side of the lake to the other, and then crossing them, they could determine the exact center or middle of the lake by noting the point of intersection; the chieftains and the one making the offering rowed to this spot on rafts made of bundles of bulrushes, or dried cattails, or logs joined and tied together to form a kind of boat large enough to hold three or four people, and also used to cross rivers where there are no bridges. With these craft they sailed to the middle of the lake and there, with special words and rites, they threw their offerings into the waters. Their gifts were of greater or lesser value according both to the request of the suppliant and his wealth, and some were so precious, as we said two chapters earlier, that the Chief

Guatavita even gilded his own body and used it as an offering, which is what the Indian reported in the city of Quito, and why the Spaniards gave this province the name of El Dorado.''

II The lust for riches drove the Spanish conquerors to obtain gold from the Indians by any means: they plundered tombs, stole objects and demanded high taxes payable in gold. The desire for gold continued throughout the Colonial period; everywhere in America foundries were built to melt down gold into negotiable coins or ingots. In 1620 Royal Mints were established in Colombia at Santa Fé and Cartagena, and there were also foundries in México, Santo Domingo, Popayán and Quito.

In the second half of the nineteenth century, as part of the then current interest in the exotic and primitive, Colombian authors like Ezequiel Uricoechea, Liborio Zerda and Vicente Restrepo investigated Precolumbian goldwork. Their books corrected earlier errors concerning indigenous goldworking techniques and established the undeniable esthetic value of the Indian objects. The development of private collections paralleled the growing number of books on Prehispanic subjects. These collections have become part of today's museums.

This increasing demand for Precolumbian gold objects stimulated treasure hunting, which even today is still responsible for the destruction of much archeological evidence. The looting of tombs in search of gold has been a common practice since the time of the Conquest. Early in the nineteenth century it became a more organized occupation and acquired what could be called ''institutionalized'' character. This was especially so in the region of Quindío, an area rich in Indian gold where looting was a common trade passed from generation to generation. The treasure hunters were a picturesque group with their own language, beliefs and superstitions.

III The complexity of Colombian geography, with its three mountain ranges, two seacoasts, immense plains and forests, gave rise to a marked regionalism among Prehispanic cultures. Coastal peoples differed from those of the highlands as well as from those of the tropical forest. Each cultural development was, at least in part, determined by the need to adapt to different environmental conditions. The unique and varied topography of Colombia, however, also permitted the coexistence of some sixty different indigenous groups all at varying stages of cultural development.

In ancient times close commercial ties existed among the indigenous cultures in Colombia. Unworked gold was a principal medium of exchange; mining centers existed from which trade routes emanated to the goldworking areas that lacked the raw material. From the rich mines of Buriticá, located in the northern portion of the modern Department of Antioquia, raw gold was sent to Sinú, Urabá, the Sierra Nevada de Santa Marta, and to Valle del Cauca. Finished gold objects were also excellent items for barter, and they were traded from Sinú, the Tairona Valley of the Sierra Nevada, and from Quindío, where gold jewelry famous for its craftsmanship was produced. The Muiscas obtained unworked gold at the popular markets of Coyaima, Natagaima, and Aipe in exchange for emeralds from Somondoco, salt mined at Zipaquirá and Nemocón, and mantles made of cotton.

IV Today it is still difficult to establish the chronological history of the Precolumbian goldworking areas of Colombia for few relative or absolute dates, such as radiocarbon dates, are available. Nevertheless, some dates have been established, for instance, on certain pieces of Muisca goldwork (920 A.D. and 645 A.D.). Other dates are associated with Tairona, Quimbaya, Calima (Yotoco) and San Agustín pottery, which indicate the existence of Precolumbian gold production as early as 1500 years before the Spanish conquest. It is significant that those sites associated with the oldest dates give evidence of highly skilled gold-working techniques such as the complex lost wax casting. Questions concerning the early stages of metals technology, however, cannot be resolved until more complete archeological information is available.

V Colombia gold ore is found in andesite formations which invariably contain gold in a free state; throughout the Central and Western Cordilleras, and in part of the Eastern Cordillera, the metal can be found in river basins and in the stratified rock formed from ancient beaches. On the Pacific slopes as a result of different geological processes, gold mixed with platinum is found in alluvial deposits. This platinum is clearly visible as surface granules on some indigenous gold objects from that area. The Museo del Oro owns five pieces made of platinum. They are small nose rings possibly made by hammering natural platinum crystals.

Silver was not used in Prehispanic Colombia. No silver artifacts have been found in Prehispanic tombs, and historical documents from the Santa Fé Mint indicate that only imported silver or silver extracted from gold was available.

The Spanish chroniclers tell us that the Indians worked copper mines located near Moniquirá and Gachalá. Copper was used in the production of gold alloys as well as for countless copper objects which date from the Prehispanic period.

Metallurgical analysis of Prehispanic gold artifacts have led to their classification in three categories according to their mixture of gold and copper. The categories are:

1) Objects of fine gold which corresponds to 22 carat gold.
2) Objects of base gold which contain a maximum of 60% gold corresponding to what is usually called 14 carat gold.
3) Objects of tumbaga which contain a maximum of 30% gold.

VI Most Precolumbian gold objects were used for personal adornment. The nose ring was the most common ornament worn by the Prehispanic peoples of Colombia. Nose ornaments were made in many different styles, ranging from the plain and simple to those that are intricately decorated. They have been found in all the archeological regions of the country. The actual composition of the metal differs considerably and the metals range from pure copper to the finest gold; there are even those made of platinum, although their number is fairly small.

Ordinary tools — chisels, needles, polishers, scrapers, fishhooks — were made of gold, as were objects of wealth and status such as golden spoons, bowls, and staves. Vessels known as "poporos," used as lime containers for the coca chewing ceremonies, were important gold objects. The delicate, long pin-like lime spatulas associated with the "poporos" are often mistaken for needles and pins. It should be also noted that many of the objects traditionally made of gold can be found represented in other media, such as stone, ceramic, and bone.

Nariño

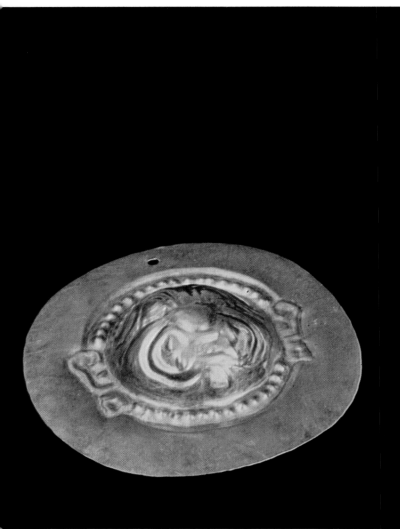

Nariño

Nariño is the name given to a cultural complex rich in archeological remains, which for the most part, has been discovered in and near the towns of Ipiales, Túquerres, Pupiales and Iles, located in the Andean region of southern Colombia. Objects made of pottery, gold, wood, stone, bone and shell have been found in some quantity. There is an abundance of pottery — cups, plates, ocarinas, globular vessels with appliquéd animal figures, and figures seated on benches.

Among the outstanding finds from this region are the objects made of cast and hammered gold which are finished in a variety of techniques, such as plating overlay, oxidation gilding, and polishing. The most common gold objects are breast plates, plaques for textile appliqués, nose rings and ear discs. Geometric designs and stylized animal forms are the most common decorative motifs. The pieces from this region clearly indicate influence from the inter-Andean cultures of Ecuador and Peru.

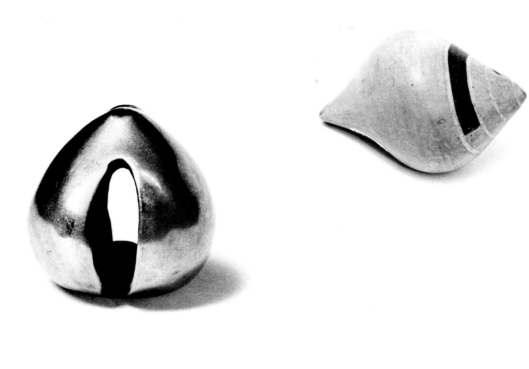

Calima

42

Calima

The Calima archeological region is located in the area of the upper Calima River on the Pacific coastal slope. Its Prehispanic inhabitants were settled farmers who lived on dispersed terraces. They commonly buried their dead in shaft tombs with lateral chambers. Calima pottery has certain very characteristic forms, such as globular vessels with three-handles, wide mouthed bowls, and anthropomorphic effigy vessels. Painted, incised, and relief decoration all occur on pottery from the Calima region.

Calima metalwork is extraordinary for its size. Nose rings, breast plates, bracelets and diadems, are made of highly polished, fine quality gold. The heads of pins are masterpieces of lost wax casting. This region is noted for the objects made of thin metal sheets joined by folds and attached by small nails to a nucleus. Major decorative devices include large masks with ear discs and nose rings, placed in the center of pectorals and other such objects. The borders of these objects will then be decorated with geometric or zoomorphic relief designs.

43

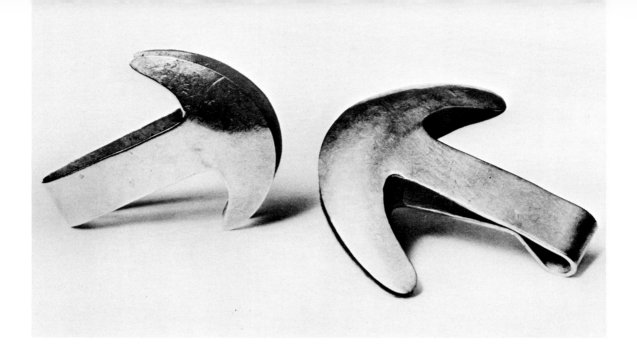

Quimbaya

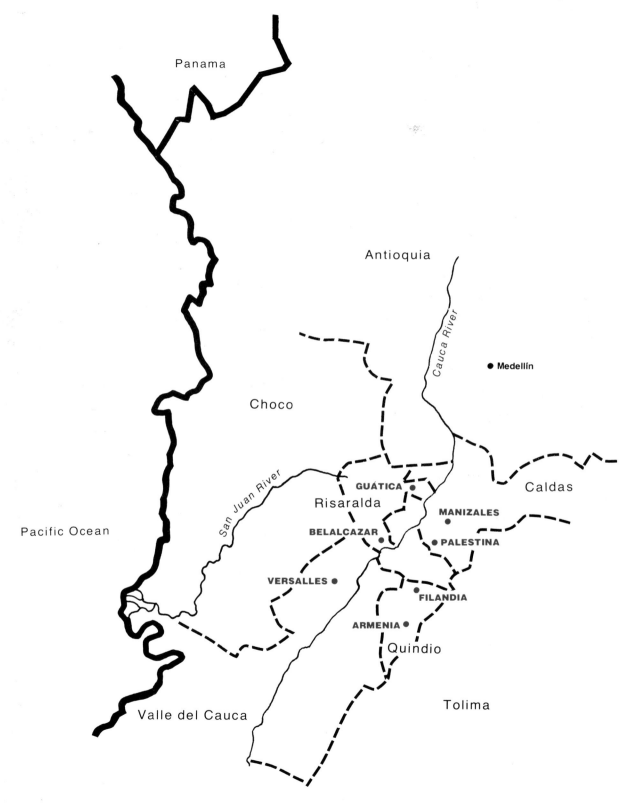

Panama

Pacific Ocean

Choco

Antioquia

Cauca River

● Medellín

San Juan River

GUÁTICA ●

Risaralda

Caldas

MANIZALES ●

BELALCAZAR ●

● PALESTINA

VERSALLES ●

● FILANDIA

ARMENIA ●

Quindio

Valle del Cauca

Tolima

Quimbaya

This extensive archeological region is located between the middle Cauca and Magdalena Rivers. It corresponds to the modern Department of Quindío and in ancient times it was the home of the Quimbaya tribe. During the Conquest these Indians were famous for the abundance of golden treasure which they possessed. Their pottery is quite varied. It includes vessels in the shape of amphoras, seals, roller and spindle whorls, zoomorphic double vessels and vessels in the form of boats and human figures. The latter are characterized by a flat, rectangular head with eyes and mouth indicated by a straight line cut into the clay. Incising, modelling and negative painting are the most common forms of decoration.

Quimbaya metalwork is the product of a highly developed technology. It also exhibits fine realism, formal proportion, and decorative simplicity and elegance. Along with pottery and gold objects, obsidian mirrors, stone axes, rock crystal beads, cotton cloth, and wooden weapons and oars, have been found in tombs.

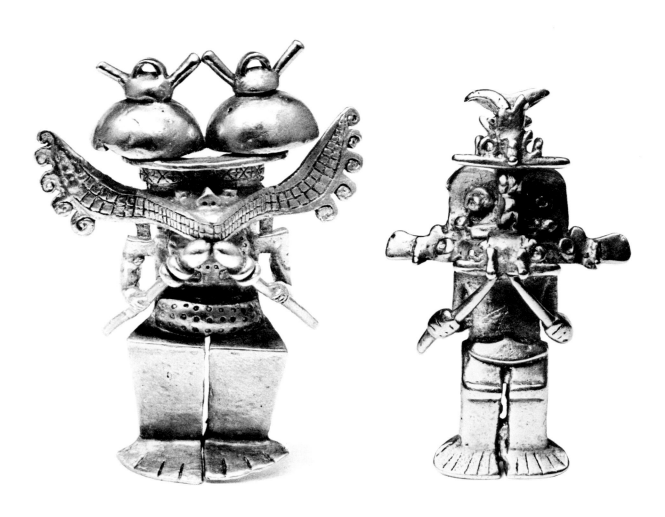

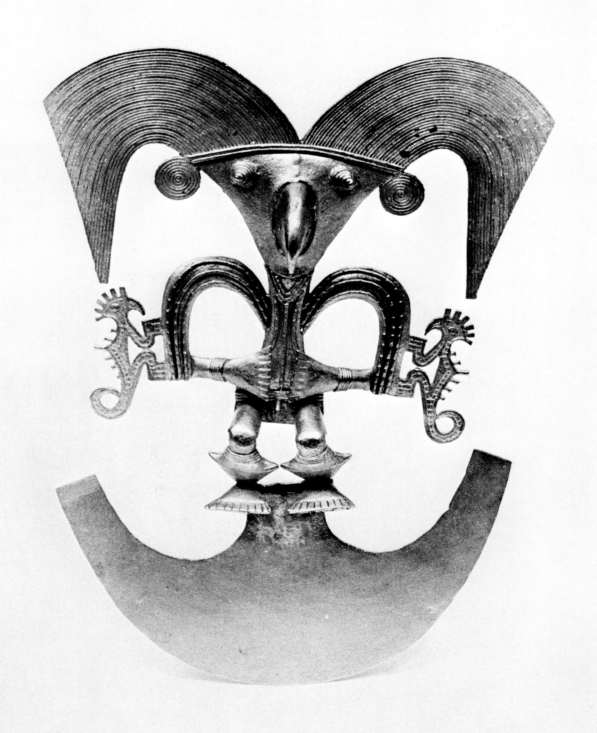

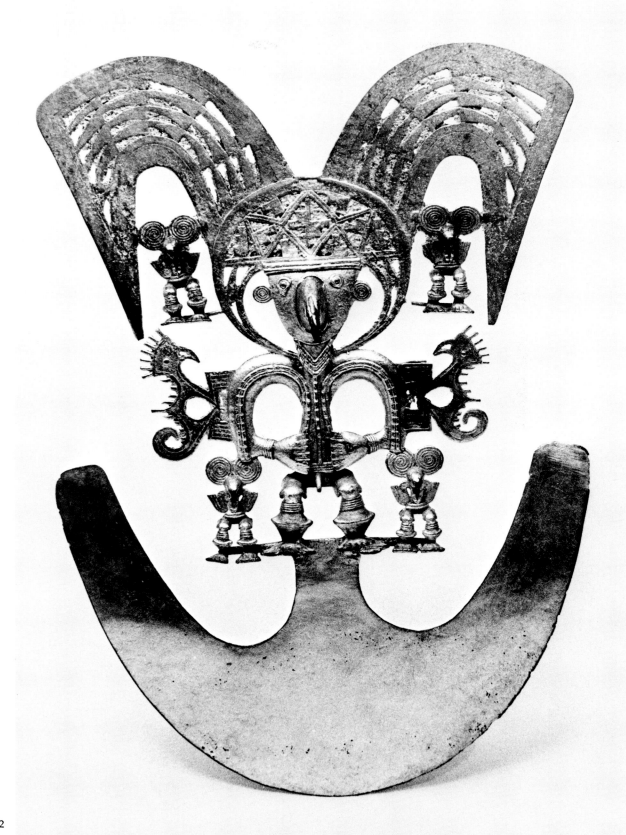

Tolima

Tolima

The Tolima archeological region is located in the Department of Tolima. The Pijaos, who lived in this area at the time of the Conquest were valiant defenders of their territory against the Spaniards. They were settled farmers who engaged in active commerce with neighboring groups, especially the Muiscas. The goldworking tradition of the Pijao had its obscure beginnings in an earlier time. Pottery similar to that found in the Cauca River Valley has been discovered in the Tolima region. Unusual pieces include miniature chairs and intricately decorated funerary urns. Characteristic ornamental designs are geometric motifs painted in many different colors.

Most of the pieces of Tolima metalwork are products of the lost wax casting method. Good quality gold is used and the pieces received a medium to high polish. Human figures of stylized flat, angular outline are typical of this group, as are stylized renderings of birds and bats.

Muisca

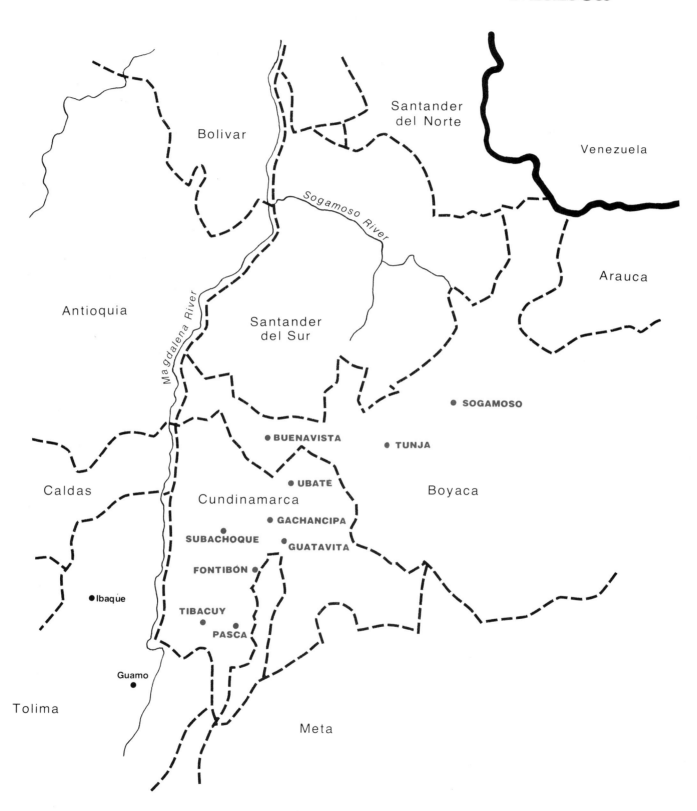

Bolivar

Santander
del Norte

Venezuela

Sogamoso River

Arauca

Antioquia

Magdalena River

Santander
del Sur

● SOGAMOSO

● BUENAVISTA

● TUNJA

Caldas

● UBATE

Boyaca

Cundinamarca

● GACHANCIPA

SUBACHOQUE ●

● GUATAVITA

FONTIBÓN ●

●Ibaque

TIBACUY ●

● PASCA

Guamo ●

Tolima

Meta

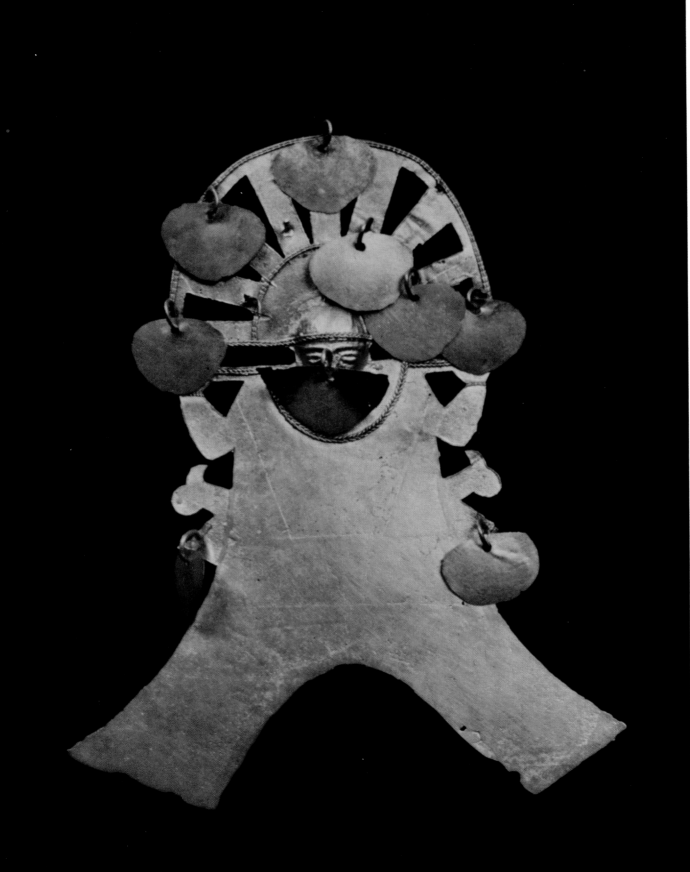

Muisca

The Muisca archeological area is located in the cold high plateau of Cundinamarca and Boyaca. Its inhabitants lived throughout the rural countryside, but some concentrations of population in villages occurred. Terrace farming, especially of corn, the staple of their diet, was practiced among the Muiscas. They were also active traders both within and without their territory. The marked social and political divisions among the Muiscas were conducive to the establishment of specialized craft guilds.

In Muisca metalwork there are a good number of tumbaga and copper objects as well as many pieces of gold. Regardless of the material, all work was roughly finished. Despite the abundance of tumbaga, few articles were gilded. Characteristic of Muisca metalwork are the *tunjos*, which are made in generalized human form. The tunjos usually show a detailed elaboration of decorative elements, and most of them indicate the sex of the figure. The principal decorative designs in Muisca goldwork are lattices with diamond or square-shaped openings, triangular fretwork, and simple, braided or spiral motifs.

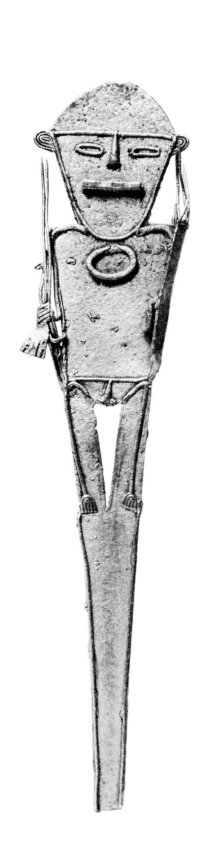

Sinú

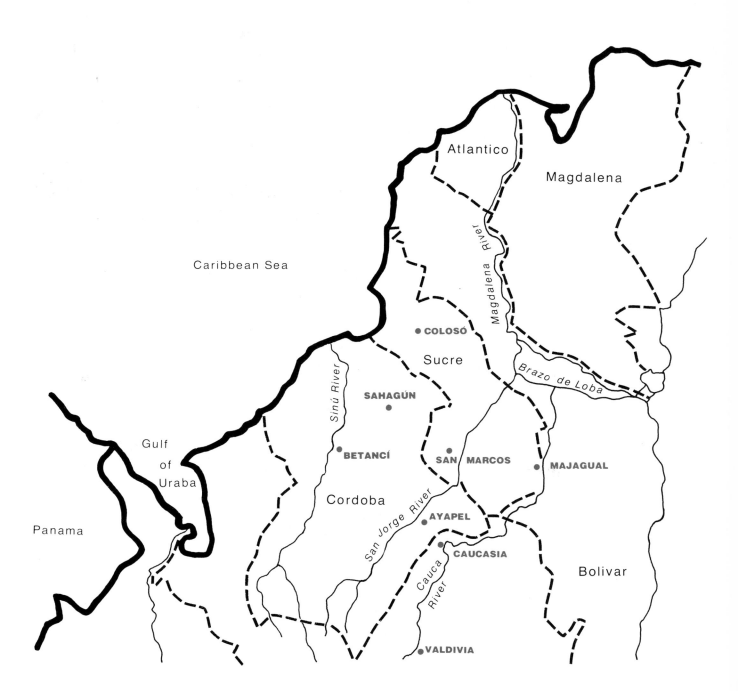

Caribbean Sea

Atlantico

Magdalena

Magdalena River

● COLOSÓ

Sucre

Brazo de Loba

Sinú River

● SAHAGÚN

Gulf
of
Uraba

● BETANCÍ

● SAN MARCOS

● MAJAGUAL

Cordoba

San Jorge River

● AYAPEL

Panama

● CAUCASIA

Bolivar

Cauca
River

● VALDIVIA

Sinú

A large area including the Sinú, San Jorge, and the Nechí River basins corresponds to the Sinú archeological region. Its inhabitants were famous in Prehispanic times for their work in gold. The ancient territory, divided into three regions called Fincenú, Pancenú, and Cenufaná, had close commerical ties to the provinces of Antioquia and Sierra Nevada de Santa Marta. Immense temples decorated with golden idols, and the mound-shaped tombs filled with rich burial furnishings were found by the Spaniards during the Conquest and it led to widespread looting of the region.

Among the objects discovered in this area are globular vessels with a bell-shaped foot, on which female figures appear in relief. Also found are tall stemmed goblets. Decoration consists of incised meander patterns.

The gold articles which come from the region are proof of the goldsmiths' great skill. The fan-shaped ear ornaments cast in false filigree are particularly notable. Decorative schemes include continuous, braided wire and depictions of reptiles and birds.

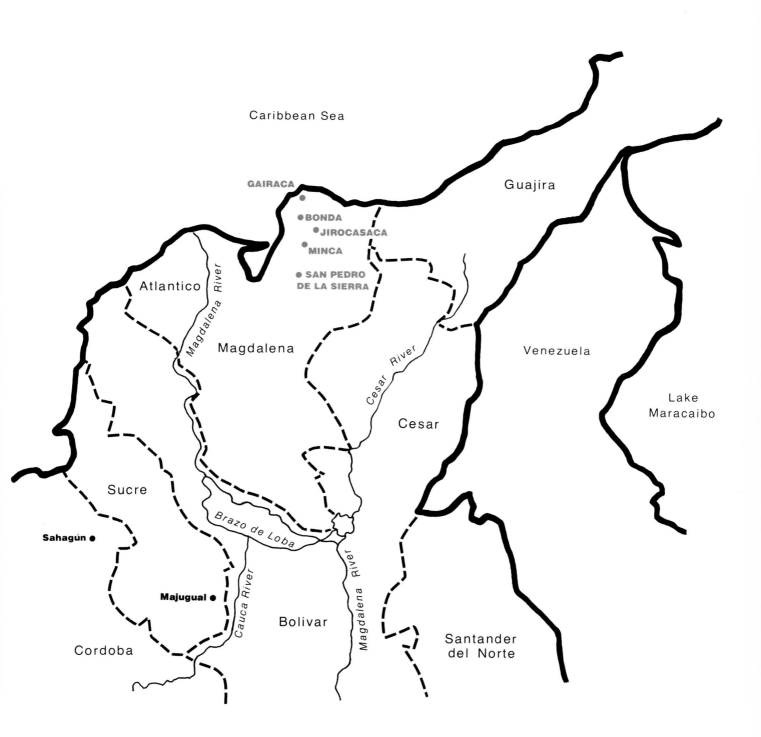

Tairona

Caribbean Sea

Guajira

GAIRACA

BONDA
JIROCASACA

MINCA

SAN PEDRO
DE LA SIERRA

Atlantico

Magdalena River

Magdalena

Venezuela

Cesar River

Lake
Maracaibo

Cesar

Sucre

Brazo de Loba

Sahagún

Cauca River

Majugual

Magdalena River

Bolivar

Santander
del Norte

Cordoba

Tairona

The Tairona lived on the lower slopes of the northern and western regions of the Sierra Nevada de Santa Marta. They had an efficiently organized social and political system. The many remnants of stone roads, bridges, floors, and stairways demonstrate their engineering and architectural skill. They built agricultural terraces and irrigation systems for a variety of crops. Corn, their basic food, was the most important. The high quality of their pottery and goldwork indicates considerable artistry and craftsmanship. The same can be said of their work in semi-precious stones, and their textiles which were used for trading with other coastal and inland peoples.

They had varying funeral customs, and the use of urns for secondary burials was common. Their magic beliefs were part of a complex religious system part of which is still current today among the indigenous people of the high Sierra.

Objects of tumbaga are abundant in this archeological region. This material is very fragile, however, and articles made of tumbaga are generally found spotted, or completely covered with a patina of copper oxide. Nevertheless, in some cases, the highly polished surfaces are still visible. An exaggerated preciosity is typical of these complicated figures. Regular geometric designs and stylized reptiles and birds are frequent decorative motifs. The influence of Central American cultures on their artistic expression, especially in ceremonial objects, is clearly evident.

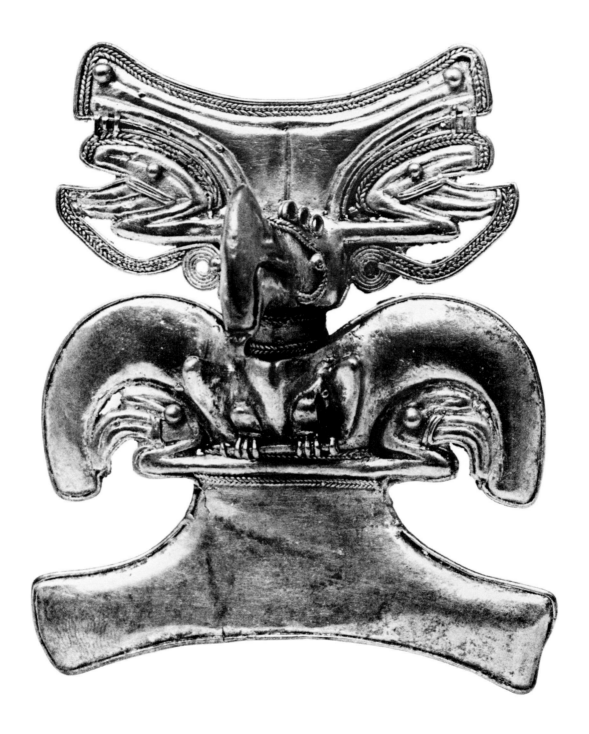

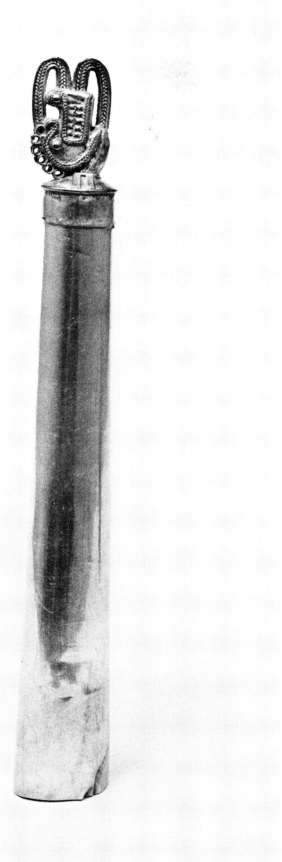

164

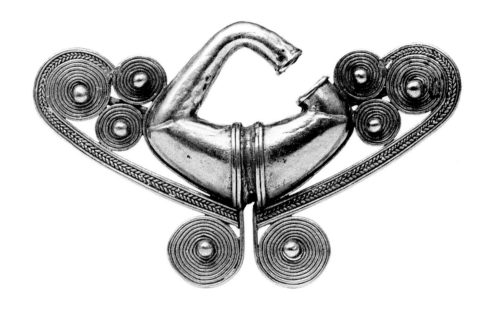

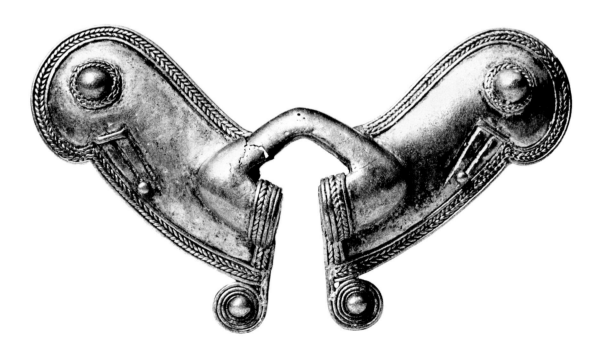

The Checklist

Provenance information is given in the following order: site, municipality, department. (A Colombian municipality is comparable to a United States county; a department to a state.) The information appears in diminishing order as it is known, i.e., if the site is unknown, municipality and department names appear; if the municipality is also unknown, only the department is indicated.

Medium is gold unless otherwise noted.

NARIÑO

1 TWO PLAQUES WITH FELINE FACES
Provenance: Pupiales, Nariño
Diameter both 9.6 cm.
Weight 25.70, 30.50 grams. (19.492, 19.493)

2 TWO PLAQUES
Provenance: Pupiales, Nariño
Diameter both 8.7 cm.
Weight 33.00, 35.70 grams. (17.753, 17.754)

3 BELL
Provenance: Pupiales, Nariño
Height 3.3 cm., width 4.0 cm.
Weight 47.40 grams. (18.650)

4 SEATED FIGURE WITH COCA IN CHEEK
Provenance: Finca Santa Lucía, Pupiales, Nariño
Ceramic, 20.0 cm. high, 11.0 cm. wide. (CN3115)

5 SHELL
Provenance: Finca San José, Ipiales, Nariño
Ceramic, 8.2 cm. high, 10.1 cm. wide. (CN3113)

CALIMA

6 CEREMONIAL REGALIA
(Contemporary reconstruction)

7 PECTORAL, STYLIZED FIGURE
Provenance: Córdoba
Height 34.6 cm., width 24.6 cm.
Weight 187.95 grams. (6371)

8 FUNERARY MASK
Provenance: Restrepo, Valle del Cauca
Height 21.2 cm., width 22.3 cm.
Weight 288.67 grams. (3308)

9 PECTORAL WITH ORNAMENTED FACE
Provenance unknown
Height 25.5 cm., width 31.5 cm.
Weight 293.50 grams. (5607)

10 PECTORAL WITH ORNAMENTED FACE
Provenance unknown
Height 35.3 cm., width 33.5 cm.
Weight 273.20 grams. (5747)

11 PECTORAL WITH ORNAMENTED FACE
Provenance unknown
Height 18.6 cm., width 19.5 cm.
Weight 126.00 grams. (6119)

12 HEADDRESS ORNAMENT
Provenance unknown
Height 28.2 cm., width 26.5 cm.
Weight 156.10 grams. (5360)

13 PAIR OF ARM ORNAMENTS
Provenance: Restrepo, Valle del Cauca
Dimensions 22.1 x 13.4 cm., 22.2 x 13.5 cm.
Weight 138.70, 133.70 grams. (5753, 5754)

14 NOSE ORNAMENT WITH DANGLES
Provenance: Restrepo, Valle del Cauca
Height 14.2 cm., width 18.0 cm.
Weight 48.25 grams. (6287)

15 NOSE ORNAMENT WITH DANGLES
Provenance unknown
Height 12.0 cm., width 14.0 cm.
Weight 33.50 grams. (5610)

16 NOSE ORNAMENT
Provenance unknown
Height 17.8 cm., width 23.6 cm.
Weight 100.52 grams. (3532)

17 NOSE ORNAMENT
Provenance unknown
Height 15.2 cm., width 20.4 cm.
Weight 82.05 grams. (3533)

18 NOSE ORNAMENT
Provenance: Restrepo, Valle del Cauca
Height 5.1 cm., width 6.9 cm.
Weight 14.60 grams. (7517)

19 PAIR OF EAR ORNAMENTS
Provenance: Anserma Neuvo, Valle del Cauca

132

Diameter 7.5 cm., 7.6 cm.
Weight 55.27, 40.42 grams. (3396, 3397)

20 TWO DIADEMS
Provenance unknown
Dimensions 63.5 x 4.0 cm., 64.0 x 3.0 cm.
Weight 83.10, 73.90 grams. (1426, 1428)

21 NECKLACE
Provenance: Restrepo, Valle del Cauca
Total length 7.60 meters; beads 0.3 cm. dm.
Total weight 139.65 grams. (4561)

22 NECKLACE, REPTILES
Provenance: Calima, Valle del Cauca
Length ornaments 5.4 cm.
Total weight 61.50 grams. (6519)

23 TEXTILE ORNAMENT
Provenance: Calarca, Quindío
Height 6.8 cm., width 9.8 cm.
Weight 12.02 grams. (2827)

24 TWO TEXTILE ORNAMENTS
Provenance unknown
Dimensions 6.5 x 10.9 cm., 6.6 x 11.0 cm.
Weight 20.00, 20.82 grams. (3562, 3563)

25 NOSE ORNAMENT WITH SIDE PLAQUE
Provenance: Minca, Santa Marta,
   Magdalena
Height 2.2 cm., plaque 5.1 cm. dm.
Weight 41.85 grams. (9659)

26 NOSE ORNAMENT WITH SIDE PLAQUE
Provenance unknown
Total width 3.6 cm.
Weight 28.35 grams. (6575)

27 NOSE ORNAMENT WITH SIDE PLAQUE
Provenance: Inzá, Cauca
Total width 3.0 cm.
Weight 30.03 grams. (130)

28 NOSE ORNAMENT
Provenance: Sahagún, Córdoba
Total width 3.0 cm.
Weight 44.40 grams. (6922)

29 NOSE ORNAMENT
Provenance: Guatica, Risaralda

Total width 2.7 cm.
Weight 32.80 grams. (9265)

30 THREE NOSE ORNAMENTS
Provenance unknown
Dimensions 2.1 x 2.5, 2.2 x 2.7, 3.0 x 3.6 cm.
Weight 52.20, 66.30, 143.00 grams. (5465,
   5467, 5471)

31 NOSE ORNAMENT
Provenance: Restrepo, Valle del Cauca
Height 1.5 cm., width 1.6 cm.
Weight 14.75 grams. (9031)

32 NOSE ORNAMENT
Provenance: Belalcazar, Risaralda
Height 1.8 cm., width 2.1 cm.
Weight 19.45 grams. (5185)

33 NOSE ORNAMENT
Provenance unknown
Height 1.5 cm., width 1.6 cm.
Weight 7.50 grams. (5771)

34 NOSE ORNAMENT
Provenance: Quindío
Height 1.3 cm., width 1.5 cm.
Weight 4.75 grams. (2553)

35 ORNAMENT
Provenance unknown
Diameter 2.2 cm.; bead 1.4 cm. long
Weight 8.50 grams. (5575)

36 TWO RINGS
Provenance unknown
Diameter 2.5 cm., 2.4 cm.

Weight 5.10, 4.75 grams. (5572, 5574)

37 TWO RINGS
Provenance unknown
Diameter 2.4 cm., 2.2 cm.
Weight 10.60, 3.40 grams. (5602, 5605)

38 TWO RINGS
Provenance unknown
Diameter 2.3 cm., 2.6 cm.
Weight 13.00, 6.50 grams. (5294, 5595)

39 BOWL
Provenance: Restrepo, Valle del Cauca
Height 6.5 cm., diameter 11.7 cm.
Weight 121.00 grams. (7528)

40 SPOON
Provenance: Restrepo, Valle del Cauca
Height 19.2 cm., width 4.4 cm.
Weight 53.00 grams. (27)

41 TWO TWEEZERS
Provenance: Restrepo, Valle del Cauca
Dimensions 5.4 x 5.2, 5.0 x 4.0 cm.
Weight 22.30, 16.45 grams. (8288, 8289)

42 POPORO (LIME CONTAINER), HUMAN FIGURE
Provenance: Restrepo, Valle del Cauca
Height 6.8 cm., width 3.6 cm.
Weight 58.80 grams. (5422)

43 PIN, CEREMONIAL FIGURE
Provenance unknown
Height 22.6 cm., width 2.1 cm.
Weight 96.55 grams. (6432)

44 PIN, BIRD STANDING ON MONKEY
Provenance: Anserma Nuevo, Valle del Cauca
Height 35.0 cm., width 2.0 cm.
Weight 109.54 grams. (3496)

45 PIN, MASKED FIGURE
Provenance: Restrepo, Valle del Cauca
Height 30.0 cm., width 2.2 cm.
Weight 130.00 grams. (26)

46 PIN, MASKED FIGURE
Provenance unknown
Height 32.7 cm., width 1.2 cm.
Weight 66.65 grams. (5233)

47 PIN, MASKED FIGURE
Provenance unknown
Height 29.6 cm., width 1.7 cm.
Weight 62.20 grams. (3453)

48 PIN, MASKED FIGURE
Provenance unknown
Height 21.5 cm., width 1.3 cm.
Weight 28.20 grams. (5300)

49 PIN, CEREMONIAL FIGURE
Provenance unknown
Height 24.6 cm., width 1.2 cm.
Weight 33.20 grams. (6164)

50 PIN, BIRD
Provenance unknown
Height 22.0 cm., width 1.7 cm.
Weight 48.34 grams. (3553)

51 PIN, BELL
Provenance: Restrepo, Valle del Cauca
Height 17.7 cm., width 1.9 cm.
Weight 24.30 grams. (13.365)

52 PIN, DOUBLE BELL
Provenance unknown
Height 30.8 cm., width 0.9 cm.
Weight 34.95 grams. (5670)

53 PIN
Provenance: Quindío
Height 24.1 cm., width 1.9 cm.
Weight 31.80 grams. (6652)

54 PIN
Provenance unknown
Height 16.5 cm., width 3.0 cm.
Weight 48.30 grams. (5762)

55 PIN
Provenance: Quindío
Height 22.5 cm., width 1.9 cm.
Weight 22.20 grams. (6650)

56 PIN
Provenance: Restrepo, Valle del Cauca
Height 32.5 cm., width 0.8 cm.
Weight 27.80 grams. (5410)

57 NOSE ORNAMENT
Provenance: Restrepo, Valle del Cauca
Diameter 2.7 cm.
Weight 18.45 grams. (8256)

58 TWO NOSE ORNAMENTS
Provenance unknown
Diameter 3.4 cm., 3.9 cm.
Weight 20.39, 30.80 grams. (683, 7022)

59 NECKLACE
Provenance: Restrepo, Valle del Cauca
Length 2.58 meters, 175 quartz beads.
Beads max. dm. 3.0 cm., max.
    width 2.0 cm. (sin no)

60 PEDESTAL BOWL
Provenance: Yotoco, Valle del Cauca
Ceramic, 28.5 cm. high, 19.3 cm. wide.
    (CY918)

61 GOURD FORM VESSEL
Provenance: Agualinda, Restrepo,

Valle del Cauca
Ceramic, 19.2 cm. high, 15.7 cm. wide.
(CC858)

62 GOURD FORM VESSEL
Provenance: Restrepo, Valle del Cauca
Ceramic, 16.0 cm. high, 9.9 cm. wide.
(CC1393)

63 STIRRUP SPOUT VESSEL, TOAD (?)
Provenance: Agualinda, Restrepo, Valle del
Cauca
Ceramic, 14.0 cm. high, 13.3 cm. wide.
(CC808)

64 STIRRUP SPOUT VESSEL, IGUANA (?)
Provenance: Restrepo, Valle del Cauca
Ceramic, 10.8 cm. high, 11.0 cm. wide.
(sin no)

65 EFFIGY VESSEL, OWL
Provenance: Vereda de Agua Mona,
Restrepo, Valle del Cauca
Ceramic, 11.3 cm. high, 12.5 wide. (CC384)

66 VESSEL WITH ZOOMORPHIC FORMS
Provenance: El Dorado, Yocoto, Valle del
Cauca
Ceramic, 10.5 cm. high, 9.6 cm. wide.
(CC394)

67 FUNERARY MASK
Provenance: Vereda Sinai, Restrepo, Valle
del Cauca
Ceramic, 14.9 cm. diameter. (CC1043)

QUIMBAYA

68 POPORO (LIME CONTAINER),
ANTHROPOMORPHIC HEAD
Provenance: Valdivia, Antioquia
Height 17.8 cm., width 13.7 cm.
Weight 319.45 grams. (3685)

69 POPORO (LIME CONTAINER) LID,
SEATED FIGURE
Provenance: Caucasia, Antioquia
Height 15.7 cm., width 6.2 cm.
Weight 166.60 grams. (6415)

70 PENDANT, STYLIZED HUMAN FIGURE
Provenance: Armenia, Quindío
Height 4.8 cm., width 2.9 cm.
Weight 19.37 grams. (3063)

71 PENDANT, STYLIZED HUMAN FIGURE
Provenance unknown
Height 8.5 cm., width 6.4 cm.
Weight 157.35 grams. (6031)

72 PENDANT, STYLIZED HUMAN FIGURE
Provenance unknown

Height 11.6 cm., width 9.5 cm.
Weight 188.85 grams. (6419)

73 PENDANT, STYLIZED FIGURE
Provenance unknown
Height 9.7 cm., width 4.3 cm.
Weight 37.10 grams. (4074)

74 PENDANT, FANTASTIC FIGURE
Provenance unknown
Height 6.2 cm., width 3.7 cm.
Weight 15.80 grams. (6025)

75 PENDANT, LIZARD
Provenance: Restrepo, Valle del Cauca
Height 30.0 cm., width 6.0 cm.
Weight 206.60 grams. (6811)

76 PENDANT, LIZARD
Provenance unknown
Height 11.3 cm., width 2.7 cm.
Weight 34.30 grams. (6010)

77 PENDANT, BUG
Provenance unknown
Height 5.8 cm., width 1.7 cm
Weight 11.50 grams. (6905)

78 PENDANT, BUG
Provenance unknown
Height 4.0 cm., width 1.9 cm.
Weight 11.80 grams. (6464)

79 ORNAMENT, HUMAN HEAD
Provenance unknown
Height 2.9 cm., width 2.3 cm.
Weight 9.30 grams. (6765)

80 BELL
Provenance unknown
Height 2.2 cm., width 2.7 cm.
Weight 13.90 grams. (5967)

81 CAP
Provenance: Restrepo, Valle del Cauca
Height 9.0 cm., diameter 18.0 cm.
Weight 247.60 grams. (7568)

82 PAIR OF EAR ORNAMENTS
Provenance: Palestina, Caldas
Diameter 6.7 cm., 6.8 cm.
Weight 125.85, 115.90 grams. (6675, 6676)

83 NECKLACE
Provenance: Versalles, Quindío
Beads 4.8 cm. long, 1.1 cm. dm.
Weight 345.00 grams. (13.090)

84 THREE FISHHOOKS
Provenance unknown
Height 5.0, 4.8, 2.4 cm.
Weight 1.67, 1.01, 0.60 grams (1822, 3132,
7452)

85 THREE FISHHOOKS
Provenance: Armenia, Quindío
Height 2.6, 3.7, 6.6 cm.
Weight 0.80, 1.25. 5.65 grams. (7918, 7920,
7924)

86 FOUR FIGURE VESSELS
Provenance unknown
Ceramic, 23.0 x 15.0 cm. (CQ558)
20.1 x 10.2 cm. (CQ571)
17.5 x 9.3 cm. (CQ594)
15.5 x 12.0 cm. (CQ600)

87 SEATED FIGURE
Provenance unknown
Ceramic, 13.9 cm. high, 11.8 cm. wide.
(CQ38)

88 JAR
Provenance: La Tigrera, Armenia, Quindío
Ceramic, 30.9 cm. high, 25.4 cm. wide.
(CQ2448)

89 JAR WITH FACE ON NECK
Provenance: Finca La Suiza, Sevilla, Valle
del Cauca
Ceramic, 20.8 cm. high, 14.7 cm. wide.
(CQ2905)

90 TWO BOWLS
Provenance unknown
Ceramic, 9.9 x 21.9 cm. (CQ48)
8.5 x 17.9 cm. (CQ474)

91 BOWL
Provenance: Montenegro, Quindío
Ceramic, 6.9 cm. high, 15.3 cm. wide.
(CQ3044)

92 PENDANT, ANTHROPOMORPHIC FIGURE
Provenance: Paletara, Coconuco, Cauca
Height 24.0 cm., width 15.8 cm.
Weight 248.67 grams. (7355)

93 PENDANT, ANTHROPOMORPHIC FIGURE
Provenance unknown
Height 16.5 cm., width 12.1 cm.
Weight 190.30 grams. (6414)

94 BOWL
Provenance: Río Guachicono, Patía, Cauca
Ceramic, 7.8 cm. high, 21.7 cm. wide.
(CCa. 2055)

TOLIMA

95 PENDANT, STYLIZED FIGURE
Provenance unknown
Height 16.0 cm., width 8.7 cm.
Weight 83.80 grams. (6418)

96 PENDANT, STYLIZED FIGURE
Provenance unknown
Height 19.0 cm., width 10.5 cm.
Weight 123.40 grams. (4661)

97 PENDANT, STYLIZED FIGURE
Provenance: Ataco, Tolima
Height 29.0 cm., width 14.4 cm.
Weight 211.60 grams. (5832)

98 TWO ORNAMENTS, ''BATS''
Provenance: Ataco, Tolima
Dimensions 7.1 x 10.7 cm., 6.9 x 10.5 cm.
Weight 55.20, 49.75 grams. (5836, 5837)

99 TWO ORNAMENTS, ''BATS''
Provenance: Ataco, Tolima
Dimensions 7.3 x 12.3 cm., 8.6 x 14.5 cm.
Weight 66.00, 113.10 grams. (5838, 5841)

100 PENDANT, FIGURE WITH ''PALMS''
Provenance: Ataco, Tolima
Height 4.2 cm., width 3.0 cm.
Weight 18.00 grams. (5881)

101 CHAIR (POSSIBLY FOR FUNERARY
BUNDLE)
Provenance: Barroso, Guamo, Tolima
Ceramic, 42.6 cm. high, 22.5 cm. wide.
(CTO.847)

MUISCA

102 ANIMAL
Provenance unknown
Height 5.7 cm., width 10.0 cm.
Weight 75.90 grams. (1115)

103 PENDANT, STYLIZED FIGURE
Provenance: Muzo, Boyacá
Height 15.4 cm., width 11.9 cm.
Weight 39.70 grams. (8512)

104 PENDANT, STYLIZED FIGURE
Provenance unknown
Height 17.2 cm., width 9.6 cm.
Weight 46.05 grams. (6184)

105 PENDANT, STYLIZED FIGURE
Provenance: Río Palomino, Magdalena
Height 16.7 cm., width 12.4 cm.
Weight 36.70 grams. (16.585)

106 PENDANT
Provenance: Buenavista, Boyacá
Height 13.6 cm., width 14.9 cm.
Weight 89.30 grams. (10.090)

107 TRIANGULAR PENDANT
Provenance: Ubaqué, Cundinamarca
Height 15.5 cm., width 17.7 cm.
Weight 63.30 grams. (7244)

108 OFFERING FIGURE (TUNJO)
Provenance unknown
Height 7.7 cm., width 3.3 cm.
Weight 24.10 grams. (3050)

109 OFFERING FIGURE (TUNJO)
Provenance unknown
Height 6.5 cm., width. 3.0 cm.
Weight 16.60 grams. (3051)

110 OFFERING FIGURE (TUNJO)
Provenance unknown
Height 10.0 cm., width 3.7 cm.
Weight 22.65 grams. (1863)

111 OFFERING FIGURE (TUNJO)
Provenance unknown
Height 13.1 cm., width 3.2 cm.
Weight 35.60 grams. (6370)

112 OFFERING FIGURE (TUNJO)
Provenance: Gachancipá, Cundinamarca
Height 12.2 cm., width 3.0 cm.
Weight 30.65 grams. (6361)

113 OFFERING FIGURE (TUNJO)
Provenance unknown
Height 14.4 cm., width 3.4 cm.
Weight 14.07 grams. (1860)

114 OFFERING FIGURE (TUNJO)
Provenance unknown
Height 10.7 cm., width 2.5 cm.
Weight 9.57 grams. (2052)

115 OFFERING FIGURE (TUNJO)
Provenance: Tibacuy, Cundinamarca
Height 12.8 cm., width 2.6 cm.
Weight 21.00 grams. (4443)

116 OFFERING FIGURE (TUNJO)
Provenance unknown
Height 12.6 cm., width 2.5 cm.
Weight 9.33 grams. (1986)

117 OFFERING FIGURE (TUNJO)
Provenance: Gachancipá, Cundinamarca
Height 15.0 cm., width 4.1 cm.
Weight 21.80 grams. (6364)

118 OFFERING FIGURE (TUNJO)
Provenance: Gachancipá, Cundinamarca
Height 12.0 cm., width 5.0 cm.
Weight 29.10 grams. (6366)

119 OFFERING FIGURE (TUNJO)
Provenance unknown
Height 5.3 cm., width 1.9 cm.
Weight 16.10 grams. (5562)

120 SNUFFING TABLET
Provenance: Guatavita, Cundinamarca
Length 10.1 cm., width 1.6 cm.

Weight 10.20 grams. (6914)

121 LIME SPATULA (FOR A POPORO)
Provenance unknown
Height 16.9 cm., width 2.6 cm.
Weight 10.23 grams. (310)

122 LIME SPATULA (FOR A POPORO)
Provenance: Sopó, Cundinamarca
Height 13.6 cm., width 3.8 cm.
Weight 31.50 grams. (181)

123 LIME SPATULA (FOR A POPORO)
Provenance: Subachoque, Cundinamarca
Height 7.1 cm,. width 4.9 cm.
Weight 17.40 grams. (6730)

124 CIRCULAR ORNAMENT
Provenance: Chaparral, Tolima
Height 7.7 cm., width 8.2 cm.
Weight 29.10 grams. (5925)

125 CIRCULAR ORNAMENT
Provenance unknown
Height 7.7 cm., width 8.6 cm.
Weight 32.20 grams. (6064)

126 PAIR OF EAR ORNAMENTS
Provenance unknown
Dimensions 6.7 x 5.2 cm., 6.5 x 5.2 cm.
Weight 6.89, 6.90 grams. (1061, 1062)

127 MOLD FOR WAX CASTING MODELS
Provenance: Tunja, Boyacá,
Stone, 7.5 cm. high, 4.2 cm. wide. (LM634)

128 MOLD FOR WAX CASTING MODELS
Provenance unknown
Stone, 5.9 cm. high, 3.6 cm. wide. (LM8)

129 CACHE VESSEL, HUMAN FIGURE
Provenance: Pasca, Cundinamarca
Ceramic, 21.2 cm. high, 13.8 cm. wide.
(CM1077)

130 CACHE VESSEL
(contents reconstructed)
Provenance: Pasca, Cundinamarca
Ceramic, 11.5 cm. high, 8.4 cm. wide.
(CM1076)

131 EFFIGY VESSEL
Provenance: Buenavista, Cundinamarca
Ceramic, 14.5 cm. high, 16.6 cm. wide.
(sin no)

132 PEDESTAL BOWL
Provenance: Fontibón, Cundinamarca
Ceramic, 14.0 cm. high, 19.6 cm. wide.
(CM2688)

133 BOTTLE WITH FACE NECK
Provenance: Encino, Santander del Sur

Ceramic, 17.9 cm. high, 15.0 cm. wide.
(CM2687)

134 BOTTLE
Provenance: Finca Primavera, Versalles,
   Quindío
Ceramic, 14.5 cm. high, 12.3 cm. wide.
(CM1226)

TAMALAMEQUE

135 FUNERARY URN
Provenance: La Quebrada Singarare area,
   Tamalameque, César
Ceramic, 78.0 cm. high, 39.0 cm. wide.
(CTam. 2034)

136 FUNERARY URN
Provenance: Sabana de Torres,
   Tamalameque, César
Ceramic, 72.7 cm. high, 37.0 cm. wide.
(CTam. 2436)

137 FUNERARY URN
Provenance: Tamalameque, César
Ceramic, 81.5 cm. high, 37.0 cm. wide.
(CTam. 1869)

SINÚ

138 FINIAL, BIRD
Provenance: Madroñal, Restrepo, Valle
   del Cauca
Height 6.0 cm., width 5.5 cm.

Weight 51.15 grams. (5668)

139 PENDANT, "FLYING FISH"
Provenance unknown
Height 4.6 cm., width 2.6 cm.
Weight 16.35 grams. (6015)

140 PENDANT, "FLYING FISH"
Provenance unknown
Height 4.6 cm., width 2.4 cm.
Weight 24.00 grams. (4805)

141 PENDANT, "FLYING FISH"
Provenance: Calima, Valle del Cauca
Height 4.0 cm., width 3.2 cm.
Weight 21.75 grams. (6401)

142 PENDANT, "FLYING FISH"
Provenance unknown
Height 3.6 cm., width 3.1 cm.
Weight 17.70 grams. (7331)

143 PENDANT, "FLYING FISH"
Provenance: Campo Hermoso, Ataco,
   Tolima
Height 3.3 cm., width 2.4 cm.
Weight 15.05 grams. (5866)

144 NECKLACE WITH BELL DANGLES
Provenance: Sinú, Córdoba
Tubular beads 4.5 x 0.8, bells 4.2 x 2.0 cm.
Total weight 184.40 grams. (6374)

145 NOSE ORNAMENT
Provenance: Río San Jorge, Córdoba
Length 32.3 cm., width 2.4 cm.
Weight 28.72 grams. (2027)

175

146 NOSE ORNAMENT
Provenance: Río Sinú, Córdoba
Length 22.8 cm., width 2.7 cm.
Weight 12.15 grams. (7809)

147 TWO NOSE ORNAMENTS
Provenance: Lorica, Córdoba
Dimensions 3.1 x 4.7 cm., 2.8 x 5.0 cm.
Weight 115.80, 103.65 grams. (16.109,
16.110)

148 PAIR OF EAR ORNAMENTS
Provenance: Guarandá, Sucre
Dimensions 4.3 x 8.1 cm., 4.3 x 8.2 cm.
Weight 17.80, 16.00 grams. (13.834, 13.835)

149 TWO EAR ORNAMENTS
Provenance: Guarandá, Sucre
Dimensions 4.4 x 8.1 cm., 4.1 x 6.6 cm.
Weight 14.00, 12.10 grams. (13.838, 13.839)

150 PENIS COVER
Provenance: Majagual, Sucre
Height 10.3 cm., width 9.6 cm.
Weight 145.60 grams. (7507)

151 FIGURE FRAGMENT
Provenance: Betancí, Córdoba
Ceramic, 12.2 cm. high, 7.8 cm. wide.
(sin no)

TAIRONA

152 NOSE ORNAMENT
Provenance: Gairaca, Santa Marta,
Magdalena
Height 5.4 cm., width 6.0 cm.
Weight 15.80 grams. (13.869)

153 NOSE ORNAMENT
Provenance: Bonda, Santa Marta,
Magdalena
Height 7.4 cm., width 10.3 cm.
Weight 61.80 grams. (13.428)

154 NOSE ORMAMENT
Provenance: San Pedro de la Sierra,
Ciénaga, Magdalena
Height 6.6 cm., width 8.0 cm.
Weight 31.05 grams. (13.560)

155 NOSE ORNAMENT
Provenance: Minca, Santa Marta,
Magdalena
Height 5.7 cm., width 8.9 cm.
Weight 24.60 grams. (11.683)

156 NOSE ORNAMENT
Provenance: San Pedro de la Sierra,
Ciénaga, Magdalena
Height 4.9 cm., width 7.1 cm.
Weight 13.15 grams. (13.462)

157 TWO NOSE ORNAMENTS
Provenance: San Pedro de la Sierra,
Ciénaga, Magdalena
Dimensions 4.4 x 8.1 cm., 4.6 x 6.6 cm.
Weight 13.20, 13.95 grams. (13.460, 13.461)

158 TWO NOSE ORNAMENTS
Provenance: Bonda, Santa Marta,
Magdalena
Dimensions 3.5 x 6.5 cm., 3.1 x 5.2 cm.
Weight 21.00, 10.15 grams. (14.011, 14.012)

159 BELL WITH FACE
Provenance: Minca, Santa Marta,
Magdalena
Height 5.2 cm., width 4.1 cm.
Weight 36.20 grams. (9895)

160 BELL WITH FACE
Provenance: Minca, Santa Marta,
Magdalena
Height 3.2 cm., width 2.9 cm.
Weight 13.50 grams. (12.832)

161 BELL WITH FACE
Provenance: Minca, Santa Marta,
Magdalena
Height 2.7 cm., width 2.3 cm.
Weight 6.95 grams. (12.835)

162 PENDANT, FANTASTIC BIRD
Provenance: Minca, Santa Marta,
Magdalena
Height 8.5 cm., width 6.8 cm.
Weight 27.40 grams. (13.184)

163 PECTORAL, THREE BIRDS
Provenance: Minca, Santa Marta,
Magdalena
Height 12.9 cm., width 12.6 cm.
Weight 42.00 grams. (13.973)

164 PENDANT, BIRD
Provenance: Guarandá, Sucre
Height 6.2 cm., width 5.5 cm.
Weight 21.60 grams. (13.831)

165 PENDANT, BIRD
Provenance: Minca, Santa Marta,
Magdalena
Height 6.0 cm., width 6.3 cm.
Weight 14.45 grams. (13.975)

166 PENDANT, FIGURE WITH BIRD
HEADDRESS
Provenance: Minca, Santa Marta,
Magdalena
Height 5.2 cm., width 4.7 cm.
Weight 15.50 grams. (11.376)

167 PENDANT, FIGURE WITH
HEADDRESS
Provenance: Girocasaca, Santa

Marta, Magdalena
Height 6.0 cm., width 5.4 cm.
Weight 27.70 grams. (11.796)

168 PECTORAL, BIRD
Provenance: San Pedro de la Sierra,
Ciénaga, Magdalena
Height 13.6 cm., width 11.7 cm.
Weight 80.70 grams. (16.791)

169 DIADEM
Provenance: Minca, Santa Marta,
Magdalena
Height 11.9 cm., length 18.6 cm.
Weight 128.40 grams. (16.014)

170 CIRCULAR PENDANT
Provenance: Bonda, Santa Marta,
Magdalena
Diameter 14.0 cm.
Weight 54.10 grams. (13.419)

171 NECKLACE, CLAWS
Provenance: Bonda, Santa Marta,
Magdalena
Claws 2.9 x 2.4 cm., carnelian beads.
Total weight 302.50 grams. (13.438)

172 NECKLACE, FROGS AS BELLS
Provenance: Minca, Santa Marta,
Magdalena
Frogs 2.5 x 1.9 cm., carnelian beads.
Total weight 78.00 grams. (13.219)

173 NECKLACE, FROGS
Provenance: Minca, Santa Marta,
Magdalena
Frogs 2.3 x 2.4 cm., carnelian beads.
Total weight 56.50 grams. (12.549)

174 ORNAMENT, FROG
Provenance: Gairaca, Santa Marta,
Magdalena
Height 4.4 cm., width 3.6 cm.
Weight 10.80 grams. (13.260)

175 PAIR OF EAR ORNAMENTS
Provenance: Minca, Santa Marta,
Magdalena
Dimensions 4.6 x 6.7 cm.,
4.5 x 6.7 cm.
Weight 30.10, 28.35 grams.
(13.987, 13.988)

176 PAIR OF ORNAMENTS
Provenance: San Pedro de la Sierra,
Ciénaga, Magdalena
Dimensions 5.0 x 6.6 cm.,
5.0 x 6.7 cm.
Weight 40.40, 45.50 grams.
(14.073, 14.074)

177 PAIR OF EAR ORNAMENTS
Provenance: Gairaca, Santa Marta,
Magdalena
Dimensions 6.6 x 8.6 cm.,
6.7 x 8.6 cm.
Weight 47.00, 48.00 grams.
(12.142, 12.143)

178 PAIR OF EAR ORNAMENTS
Provenance: San Pedro de la Sierra,
Ciénaga, Magdalena
Dimensions 6.2 x 8.1 cm.,
6.4 x 8.3 cm.
Weight 52.70, 51.50 grams.
(13.554, 13.555)

179 NOSE ORNAMENT
Provenance: Betancí, Córdoba
Length 10.4 cm., width 1.7 cm.
Weight 22.95 grams. (13.541)

180 TWO NOSE ORNAMENTS
Provenance: Bonda, Santa Marta,
Magdalena
Dimensions 2.2 x 5.7 cm.,
2.2 x 5.5 cm.
Weight 6.60, 7.80 grams.
(13.519, 13.520)

181 TWO NOSE ORNAMENTS
Provenance: Bonda, Santa Marta,
Magdalena
Dimensions 3.6 x 7.6 cm.,
3.3 x 6.6 cm.
Weight 12.15, 9.20 grams.
(13.432, 13.433)

182 NOSE ORNAMENT
Provenance: San Pedro de la Sierra,
Ciénaga, Magdalena
Height 5.1 cm., width 10.7 cm.
Weight 14.65 grams. (14.096)

183 NOSE ORNAMENT
Provenance: Bonda, Santa Marta,
Magdalena
Height 6.5 cm., width 12.2 cm.
Weight 24.90 grams. (13.785)

184 EAR PLUG
Provenance: Minca, Santa Marta,
Magdalena
Length 18.2 cm., width 2.0 cm.
Weight 15.20 grams. (13.991)

185 EAR PLUG
Provenance: Minca, Santa Marta,
Magdalena
Length 15.9 cm., width 2.2 cm.
Weight 14.25 grams. (13.993)

186 EAR PLUG ORNAMENT
Provenance: Minca, Santa Marta,
Magdalena
Height 3.4 cm., width 5.6 cm.
Weight 16.50 grams. (11.054)

187 TWO NOSE ORNAMENTS
Provenance: Minca, Santa Marta,
Magdalena
Dimensions 2.1 x 2.4 cm.,
2.4 x 2.9 cm.
Weight 13.70, 48.35 grams.
(13.720, 15.705)

188 SPIRAL ORNAMENT
Provenance: Minca, Santa Marta,
Magdalena
Height 8.7 cm., width 17.2 cm.
Weight 42.50 grams. (13.228)

189 SPIRAL ORNAMENT
Provenance: Palmarito, Magdalena
Height 7.2 cm., width 15.6 cm.
Weight 38.30 grams. (15.029)

190 SPIRAL ORNAMENT
Provenance: Bonda, Santa Marta,
Magdalena
Gilt copper, 8.9 cm. high, 18.4 cm.
wide.
Weight 27.35 grams. (13.755)

191 LIP PLUG
Provenance: Minca, Santa Marta,
Magdalena
Stone, 2.8 cm. high, 3.9 cm. wide.
(LT644)

192 LIP PLUG
Provenance: Minca, Santa Marta,
Magdalena
Stone, 2.4 cm. high, 2.8 cm. wide.
(LT646)

193 ARM ORNAMENT FOR
CEREMONIAL DANCE
Provenance: Minca, Santa Marta,
Magdalena
Stone, 5.3 cm. high, 40.2 cm. wide.
LT355)

194 ARM ORNAMENT FOR
CEREMONIAL DANCE
Provenance: Minca, Santa Marta,
Magdalena
Stone, 3.9 cm. high, 27.7 cm. wide.
(LT393)

195 ARM ORNAMENT FOR
CEREMONIAL DANCE

Provenance: Minca, Santa Marta,
Magdalena
Stone, 3.3 cm. high, 24.8 cm. wide.
(LT544)

196 GOLDWORKING ANVIL
Provenance unknown
Stone, 5.6 cm. high, 12.5 cm. wide.
(LT757)

197 GOLDWORKING HAMMER
Provenance: Colosó, Sucre
Stone, 3.3 cm. high, 2.9 cm. wide.
(LS373)

198 EFFIGY VESSEL
Provenance: Bonda, Santa Marta,
Magdalena
Ceramic, 25.8 cm. high, 18.0 cm.
wide. (CT1536)

199 OCARINA
Provenance: Bonda, Santa Marta,
Magdalena
Ceramic, 6.2 cm. high, 5.2 cm.
wide. (CT1514)

200 OCARINA
Provenance: Minca, Santa Marta,
Magdalena
Ceramic, 7.5 cm. high, 4.4 cm.
wide. (CT2310)

201 CACHE VESSEL
Provenance: El Pueblito, Santa
Marta, Magdalena
Ceramic, 47.5 cm. high, 18.3 cm.
wide. (CT1621)

202 CACHE VESSEL CONTAINING
CARNELIAN BEADS
(Contents reconstructed)
Provenance: El Pueblito, Santa
Marta, Magdalena
Ceramic, 10.0 cm. high, 11.0 cm.
wide. (CT1625)

203 PEDESTAL BOWL
Provenance: San Pedro de la Sierra,
Ciénaga, Magdalena
Ceramic, 12.1 cm. high, 15.8 cm.
wide. (CT1745)

204 PEDESTAL BOWL
Provenance: Río de Piedra, Santa
Marta, Magdalena
Ceramic, 9.0 cm. high, 13.3 cm.
wide. (CT910)